Interactive Learning Guide for Students

Nutrition Now

SIXTH EDITION

Judith Brown, R. D, M.P.H., Ph.D.

Professor Emerita
University of Minnesota

Prepared by

Jennifer Koslo
Glendale Community College

WADSWORTH
CENGAGE Learning

Australia • Brazil • Japan • Korea • Mexico • Singapore • Spain • United Kingdom • United States

For product information and technology assistance, contact us at **Cengage Learning Customer & Sales Support, 1-800-354-9706**

For permission to use material from this text or product, submit all requests online at **www.cengage.com/permissions** Further permissions questions can be emailed to **permissionrequest@cengage.com**

ISBN-13: 978-0-538-73997-9
ISBN-10: 0-538-73997-5

Wadsworth
20 Davis Drive
Belmont, CA 94002-3098
USA

Cengage Learning is a leading provider of customized learning solutions with office locations around the globe, including Singapore, the United Kingdom, Australia, Mexico, Brazil, and Japan. Locate your local office at: **www.cengage.com/global**

Cengage Learning products are represented in Canada by Nelson Education, Ltd.

To learn more about Wadsworth, visit **www.cengage.com/wadsworth**

Purchase any of our products at your local college store or at our preferred online store **www.ichapters.com**

Printed in the United States of America
2 3 4 5 6 7 13 12 11

Table of Contents

Welcome to your interactive learning guide! In the **Study Tools** section of this workbook you will find the following study aids for each unit of *Nutrition Now*, 6th edition:

- a list of key concepts,
- a brief outline,
- a list of any key terms with definitions, and
- a multiple-choice practice test.

An answer key for each practice test is also included. (You may not be using all 33 of these units in your nutrition course.)

Your instructor may ask you to complete assignments from the **Worksheets** section of this workbook.[1]

Study Tools 1
Unit 1 – Key Nutrition Concepts and Terms 1
Unit 2 – The Inside Story about Nutrition and Health 7
Unit 3 – Ways of Knowing about Nutrition 13
Unit 4 – Understanding Food and Nutrition Labels 19
Unit 5 – Nutrition, Attitudes, and Behavior...24
Unit 6 – Healthy Diets, Dietary Guidelines, MyPyramid and More 29
Unit 7 – How the Body Uses Food: Digestion and Absorption 34
Unit 8 – Calories! Food, Energy, and Energy Balance 40
Unit 9 – Obesity to Underweight: The Highs and Lows of Weight Status............45
Unit 10 – Weight Control: The Myths and Realities 51
Unit 11 – Disordered Eating: Anorexia Nervosa, Bulimia, and Pica.....................56
Unit 12 – Useful Facts about Sugars, Starches, and Fiber 61
Unit 13 – Diabetes Now 67
Unit 14 – Alcohol: The Positives and Negatives..73
Unit 15 – Proteins and Amino Acids 78
Unit 16 – Vegetarian Diets 83
Unit 17 – Food Allergies and Intolerances 88
Unit 18 – Fats and Cholesterol in Health..94
Unit 19 – Nutrition and Heart Disease 100
Unit 20 – Vitamins and Your Health..105
Unit 21 – Phytochemicals and Genetically Modified Food....................................110
Unit 22 – Diet and Cancer 115

---

[1] <u>Note to instructors</u>: These worksheets are designed to accompany the exercises presented in the *Interactive Learning Guide for Instructors* available for *Nutrition Now*, 6th edition (ISBN 0538734191)

Unit 23 – Good Things to Know about Minerals..120
Unit 24 – Dietary Supplements and Functional Foods..126
Unit 25 – Water Is an Essential Nutrient 131
Unit 26 – Nutrient-Gene Interactions in Health and Disease..136
Unit 27 – Nutrition and Physical Fitness for Everyone 142
Unit 28 – Nutrition and Physical Performance..147
Unit 29 – Good Nutrition for Life: Pregnancy, Breastfeeding, and Infancy 153
Unit 30 – Nutrition for the Growing Years: Childhood through Adolescence...................159
Unit 31 – Nutrition and Health Maintenance for Adults of All Ages 164
Unit 32 – The Multiple Dimensions of Food Safety 169
Unit 33 – Aspects of Global Nutrition..174

Worksheets...179
Worksheet 1—Family Tree Health History..179
Worksheet 2—Creating Your Own Fraudulent Nutrition Product....................................181
Worksheet 3—Cultural Influences on Food Preferences Interview Form..........................183
Worksheet 5—Behavioral Change Plan Activity 185
Worksheet 7—Portion Size Recording Form 187
Worksheet 8—Dietary Assessment Assignment..189
Worksheet 9—Physical Activity Assessment 201
Worksheet 10—Anthropometry Lab...203
Worksheet 12—Assessing Calcium Intake..207
Worksheet 13—Should Herbs Be Regulated as Drugs? 209
Worksheet 15A—Child Nutrition Dilemmas 1 211
Worksheet 15B—Child Nutrition Dilemmas 2 213

Unit 1 – Key Nutrition Concepts and Terms

Key Concepts

- At the core of the science of nutrition are concepts that represent basic "truths" and serve as the foundation of our understanding about normal nutrition.
    1. Food is a basic need of humans.
    2. Foods provide energy (calories), nutrients, and other substances needed for growth and health.
    3. Health problems related to nutrition originate within cells.
    4. Poor nutrition can result from both inadequate and excessive levels of nutrient intake.
    5. Humans have adaptive mechanisms for managing fluctuations in nutrient intake.
    6. Malnutrition can result from poor diets and from disease states, genetic factors, or combinations of these causes.
    7. Some groups of people are at higher risk of becoming inadequately nourished than others.
    8. Poor nutrition can influence the development of certain chronic diseases.
    9. Adequacy, variety, and balance are key characteristics of a healthy diet.
    10. There are no "good" or "bad" foods.
- Most nutrition concepts relate to nutrients.

Unit Outline

I. The meaning of nutrition
   A. Nutrition defined
      1. Nutrition is a "melting pot" science
      2. Nutrition knowledge is applicable
II. Foundation knowledge for thinking about nutrition
   A. Food is a basic need of humans
      1. Food terrorism
   B. Foods provide energy (calories), nutrients, and other substances needed for growth and health
      1. Calories
      2. Nutrients
      3. Other substances in food
   C. Some nutrients must be provided by the diet
   D. Our requirements for essential nutrients
   E. Nutrient intake standards
      1. Dietary Reference Intakes (DRIs)
      2. Adequate Intakes and Estimated Average Requirements
      3. Tolerable Upper Intake Levels
      4. Revising the DRIs
   F. Health problems related to nutrition originate within cells
   G. Nutrient functions at the cellular level
   H. Poor nutrition can result from both inadequate and excessive levels of nutrient intake
   I. Steps in the development of nutrient deficiencies and toxicities
      1. Nutrient deficiencies are often multiple
      2. The "ripple effect"
   J. Humans have adaptive mechanisms for managing fluctuations in nutrient intake
   K. Malnutrition can result from poor diets and from disease states, genetic factors, or combinations of these factors
   L. Some groups of people are at higher risk of becoming inadequately nourished than others
   M. Poor nutrition can influence the development of certain chronic diseases
   N. Adequacy, variety, and balance are key characteristics of a healthful diet

2

    O. Energy and nutrient density
    P. There are no "good" or "bad" foods

Unit Glossary

- **nutrition:** The study of foods, their nutrients and other chemical constituents, and the effects that food constituents have on health.
- **food security:** Access at all times to a sufficient supply of safe, nutritious foods.
- **food insecurity:** Limited or uncertain availability of safe, nutritious foods—or the ability to acquire them in socially acceptable ways.
- **calorie:** A unit of measure of the amount of energy supplied by food. (Also known as a kilocalorie, or the "large Calorie" with a capital C.)
- **nutrients:** Chemical substances in food that are used by the body for growth and health. The six categories of nutrients are carbohydrates, proteins, fats, vitamins, minerals, and water.
- **phytochemicals** (phyto = plant): Chemical substances in plants. Some phytochemicals perform important functions in the human body. They give plants color and flavor, participate in processes that enable plants to grow, and protect plants against insects and diseases. Also called phytonutrients.
- **antioxidants:** Chemical substances that prevent or repair damage to cells caused by exposure to oxidizing agents such as environmental pollutants, smoke, ozone, and oxygen. Oxidation reactions are a normal part of cellular processes.
- **essential nutrients:** Substances required for normal growth and health that the body can generally not produce, or not produce in sufficient amounts. Essential nutrients must be obtained in the diet.
- **nonessential nutrients:** Nutrients required for normal growth and health that the body can manufacture in sufficient quantities from other components of the diet. We do not require a dietary source of nonessential nutrients.
- **metabolism:** The chemical changes that take place in the body. The formation of energy from carbohydrates is an example of a metabolic process.
- **malnutrition:** Poor nutrition resulting from an excess or lack of calories or nutrients.
- **chronic diseases:** Slow-developing, long-lasting diseases that are not contagious (for example, heart disease, diabetes, and cancer). They can be treated but not always cured.
- **energy-dense foods:** Foods that provide relatively high levels of calories per unit weight of the food. Fried chicken; cheeseburgers; a biscuit, egg, and sausage sandwich; and potato chips are energy-dense foods.
- **empty-calorie foods:** Foods that provide an excess of energy or calories in relation to nutrients. Soft drinks, candy, sugar, alcohol, and animal fats are considered empty-calorie foods.
- **nutrient-dense foods:** Foods that contain relatively high amounts of nutrients compared to their calorie value. Broccoli, collards, bread, cantaloupe, and lean meats are examples of nutrient-dense foods.

Practice Multiple-Choice Test

1. Characteristics of food insecure households include of the following EXCEPT:
    a. female-headed households.
    b. families with young children who are poor.
    c. poor families who live in inner cities.
    d. families who live in the midwest.

2. Phytochemicals have all of the following characteristics EXCEPT:
   a. there are over 2000 of them in meats.
   b. they give plants their color.
   c. a diet high in phytochemicals is related to lower risks of developing certain cancers.
   d. an example of a phytochemical is allin.

3. Essential nutrients:
   a. can be manufactured by the body.
   b. must be obtained through the diet.
   c. include glucose and cholesterol.
   d. are required in the same amounts by everyone.

4. All of following describe the Dietary Reference Intakes (DRIs) EXCEPT:
   a. they are nutrient levels based on age, gender, and ethnicity.
   b. they recommend intake levels of essential nutrients and safe upper levels of intake.
   c. they are meant to meet the nutrient needs of almost all healthy people.
   d. they include the RDAs, AIs, EARs, and the ULs.

5. The most common cell in the body is:
   a. the white blood cell.
   b. the amino acid.
   c. the red blood cell.
   d. glucose.

6. Malnutrition is best described as:
   a. too few calories.
   b. too few nutrients.
   c. an excess of calories.
   d. an excess or lack of calories or nutrients.

7. A deficiency results when:
   a. the intake of a nonessential nutrient is inadequate for a prolonged time.
   b. excessively high intakes of a nutrient are ingested.
   c. a person does not eat enough oranges.
   d. the intake of an essential nutrient is inadequate for a prolonged time.

8. An example of a nutrient-dense food is:
   a. a double cheeseburger.
   b. cantaloupe.
   c. sports drinks.
   d. potato chips.

9. All of the following describe the science of nutrition EXCEPT:
   a. It is the study of foods and health.
   b. It examines the effect of chemical constituents on body processes.
   c. It is an interdisciplinary science.
   d. The study of nutrition uses subjective methods.

4

10. Knowledge of how food preferences develop and change is obtained by the following scientific methods:
    a. biological studies.
    b. chemical studies.
    c. food science.
    d. behavioral and social sciences.

11. *Food security* refers to all of the following EXCEPT:
    a. access to safe food.
    b. access to enough food.
    c. eating meals at a soup kitchen less than once a month.
    d. the ability to obtain food in a socially acceptable way.

12. *Food insecurity* refers to all of the following EXCEPT:
    a. lack of cooking skills.
    b. limited money for grocery shopping.
    c. lack of transportation for obtaining food.
    d. limited supply of nutritious foods.

13. Rates of overweight, heart disease, and diabetes are higher in which of the following populations?
    a. Adults who are food secure and poor
    b. Adults who are food secure and wealthy
    c. Adults who are food insecure and poor
    d. Adults who are food insecure and wealthy

14. Food terrorism is a relatively new phenomenon which refers to the following:
    a. foods that contain large amounts of saturated fats.
    b. intentional contamination of the food or water supply.
    c. pesticides in foods.
    d. hormone use in cattle.

15. All of the following have the potential to spread illness in the food supply EXCEPT:
    a. botulism.
    b. ricin.
    c. *E. coli* 0517:H7.
    d. phytates.

16. A calorie is defined as:
    a. a substance present in food.
    b. a nutrient.
    c. fattening.
    d. a unit of measure of the amount of energy in a food.

17. A nutrient is defined as:
    a. a unit of measure of the amount of energy in a food.
    b. the amount of heat released during digestion of food.
    c. the fibrous part of a plant.
    d. a chemical substance present in food that is used by the body.

18. What are the major categories of nutrients for humans?
    a. Carbohydrates, fiber, proteins, fats, and water.
    b. Carbohydrates, proteins, fats, vitamins, and minerals.
    c. Carbohydrates, proteins, fats, vitamins, minerals, and water.
    d. Carbohydrates, proteins, fats, vitamins, minerals, and fiber.

19. Carbohydrates include all of the following EXCEPT:
    a. simple sugars.
    b. starches.
    c. fiber.
    d. fat.

20. Proteins are a class of nutrients made up of the following:
    a. 9 fatty acids.
    b. 11 fatty acids.
    c. 20 amino acids.
    d. 29 amino acids.

21. All of the following describe the fats nutrient category EXCEPT:
    a. fats include *trans* fats.
    b. fats are both saturated and unsaturated.
    c. fats are soluble in water.
    d. fats include cholesterol.

22. Characteristics of vitamins include all of the following EXCEPT:
    a. too many can be harmful for the body.
    b. they include water-soluble and fat-soluble vitamins.
    c. they include 35 known substances.
    d. they perform specific functions in the body.

23. All of the following are true regarding minerals EXCEPT:
    a. they include 15 known substances.
    b. they are found in the ash left when a food is burned.
    c. they are required for optimal health in humans.
    d. they include fat-soluble and water-soluble minerals.

24. The following nutrients supply energy in the diet:
    a. carbohydrates, vitamins, fats, and proteins.
    b. carbohydrates, vitamins, fat, proteins, and minerals.
    c. carbohydrates, fats, and proteins.
    d. carbohydrates, fats, proteins, vitamins, minerals, and water.

25. The body obtains energy from proteins, fats, and carbohydrates by a process called:
    a. adaptation.
    b. the "ripple effect."
    c. free radicalism.
    d. metabolism.

6

26. The body's mechanisms to protect against fluctuations in nutrient intake include all of the following EXCEPT:
    a. lowering of the body's energy expenditure.
    b. increased absorption of the nutrient.
    c. a craving for the missing nutrient.
    d. an ability to excrete the excess in urine.

27. Which of the following groups need the highest amounts of nutrients?
    a. Pregnant and breastfeeding women
    b. Teenage boys
    c. People who live in colder climates
    d. Women who are middle aged

28. Characteristics of a healthy diet include all of the following EXCEPT:
    a. variety.
    b. balance.
    c. adequacy.
    d. empty calorie.

29. A chronic disease:
    a. is contagious.
    b. develops slowly over time due to a poor diet.
    c. is easily cured.
    d. is not affected by diet.

30. Foods can be divided into the following categories:
    a. "good" and "bad."
    b. "everyday" foods and "occasional" foods.
    c. "fattening" and "negative calorie."
    d. calorie dense and empty calorie.

To check yourself, use the answer key at the bottom of the page.[2]

_____

[2] 1. d, 2. a, 3. b, 4. a, 5. c, 6. d, 7. d, 8. b, 9. d, 10. d, 11. c, 12. a, 13. c, 14. b, 15. d, 16. d, 17. d, 18. c, 19. d, 20. c, 21. c, 22. c, 23. d, 24. c, 25. d, 26. c, 27. a, 28. d, 29. b, 30. b

Unit 2 – The Inside Story about Nutrition and Health

Key Concepts

- Health and longevity are affected by diet. Other lifestyle behaviors, genetic traits, the environment to which we are exposed, and access to quality health care also affect health and longevity.
- Dramatic changes in the types of foods consumed by modern humans compared with early humans are related in some ways to the development of today's leading health problems.
- The diets and health of Americans are periodically evaluated by national studies.
- The health status of a population changes for the better or worse as diets change for the better or worse.

Unit Outline

I. Nutrition in the context of overall health
    A. The nutritional state of the nation
        1. Shared dietary risk factors
        2. Chronic inflammation and oxidative stress
        3. Nutrient-gene interactions and health
    B. The importance of food choices
II. Diet and diseases of western civilization
    A. Our bodies haven't changed
        1. Then...
        2. ...and now
    B. Changing diets, changing disease rates
    C. The power of prevention
III. Improving the American diet
    A. What should we eat?
    B. Nutrition surveys: tracking the American diet

Unit Glossary

- **chronic diseases:** Slow-developing, long-lasting diseases that are not contagious (for example, heart disease, cancer, diabetes). They can be treated but not always cured.
- **diabetes:** A disease characterized by abnormal utilization of glucose by the body and elevated blood glucose levels. There are three main types of diabetes: type 1, type 2, and gestational diabetes. The word diabetes in this text refers to type 2 diabetes, by far the most common. Diabetes is short for the term "diabetes mellitus."
- **hypertension:** High blood pressure. It is defined as blood pressure exerted inside of blood vessel walls that typically exceeds 140/90 mm Hg (or, millimeters of mercury).
- **stroke:** The event that occurs when a blood vessel in the brain suddenly ruptures or becomes blocked, cutting off blood supply to a portion of the brain. Stroke is often associated with "hardening of the arteries" in the brain. (Also called a cerebral vascular accident.)
- **Alzheimer's disease:** A brain disease that represents the most common form of dementia. It is characterized by memory loss for recent events that expands to more distant memories over the course of five to ten years. It eventually produces profound intellectual decline characterized by dementia and personal helplessness.
- **chronic inflammation:** Low-grade inflammation that lasts weeks, months, or years. Inflammation is the first response of the body's immune system to infectious agents, toxins, or irritants. It triggers the release of biologically active substances that promote oxidation and other reactions to counteract the

8

infection, toxin, or irritant. A side-effect of chronic inflammation is that it also damages lipids, cells, and tissues.

- **oxidative stress:** A condition that occurs when cells are exposed to more oxidizing molecules (such as free radicals) than to antioxidant molecules that neutralize them. Over time, oxidative stress causes damage to lipids, DNA, cells and tissues. It increases the risk of heart disease, type 2 diabetes, cancer, and other diseases.
- **osteoporosis:** A condition in which bones become fragile and susceptible to fracture due to a loss of calcium and other minerals.
- **free radicals:** Chemical substances (often oxygen-based) that are missing electrons. The absence of electrons makes the chemical substance reactive and prone to oxidizing nearby molecules by stealing electrons from them. Free radicals can damage lipids, proteins, DNA (genetic material contained in cells), cells, and tissues by altering their chemical structure and functions.
- **antioxidants:** Chemical substances that prevent or repair damage to cells caused by oxidizing agents such as pollutants, ozone, smoke, and reactive oxygen. Oxidation reactions are a normal part of cellular processes. Vitamins C and E and certain phytochemicals function as antioxidants.

Practice Multiple-Choice Test

1. Which of the following are the major contributors to death among adults under the age of 75 years in the United States? (Choose the best answer.)
   a. Access to healthcare, lifestyle factors
   b. Access to healthcare, lifestyle factors, genetic makeup, environmental factors
   c. Education, access to healthcare, lifestyle factors, genetic makeup
   d. Education, lifestyle factors, genetic makeup, environmental factors

2. The leading causes of hospitalization in children in the United States in the 1930s:
   a. were the same as they are today.
   b. were related to chronic diseases such as hypertension.
   c. were related to vitamin D deficiency and niacin deficiency.
   d. were related to low iron intake.

3. Over half of all Americans die from which two diseases?
   a. Diabetes and HIV
   b. Diabetes and heart disease
   c. Diabetes and cancer
   d. Heart disease and cancer

4. If given access to the type of food choices available in the United States, people tend to choose a diet which is:
   a. high in animal fat, high in complex carbohydrates, and low in fruits and vegetables.
   b. moderate in animal fat, low in complex carbohydrates, and low in fruits and vegetables.
   c. high in animal fat, low in complex carbohydrates, and low in fruits and vegetables.
   d. low in animal fat, high in processed foods, low in vegetables, and high in salt.

5. Foods most likely consumed by hunter-gatherers are:
   a. rice, yogurt, and pork.
   b. carrots, nuts, and fish.
   c. wheat, olive oil, and chicken eggs.
   d. sugar, wild cucumbers, and roots.

6. Adoption of a Western diet by people immigrating to the United States is associated with which of the following?
    a. Increased rate of diabetes, increased fat intake, decreased fiber intake
    b. Increased iron intake, increased fat and calorie intake
    c. Increased rate of diabetes, increased fat intake, increased fruit and vegetable intake
    d. Increased rate of diabetes, increased fat intake, increased fiber intake

7. What does the MyPyramid Food Guide recommend?
    a. Consumption of adequate discretionary calories each day
    b. Consumption of basic foods like whole milk, hamburger, and potatoes
    c. Consumption of nutrient-dense forms of basic foods
    d. Consumption of only white or green vegetables

8. All of the following are considered lifestyle factors that affect health EXCEPT:
    a. diet.
    b. smoking habits.
    c. stress level.
    d. gender.

9. Diet quality affects the development of all of the following EXCEPT:
    a. heart disease.
    b. HIV/AIDS.
    c. diabetes.
    d. cancer.

10. Chronic diseases have all of the following characteristics EXCEPT:
    a. they are slow to develop.
    b. they are always curable.
    c. they are long lasting.
    d. they are treatable.

11. The most common nutritional disorder in the United States is:
    a. high sodium levels.
    b. vitamin C deficiency.
    c. obesity.
    d. rickets.

12. Overweight increases the likelihood of developing all of the following EXCEPT:
    a. hypertension.
    b. certain types of cancer.
    c. alcoholic cirrhosis.
    d. diabetes.

13. Hypertension is linked to which of the following two diseases?
    a. Cancer and heart disease
    b. Stroke and heart disease
    c. Osteoporosis and cancer
    d. Stroke and diabetes

14. Low fruit and vegetable intake is related to all of the following conditions EXCEPT:
    a. iron-deficiency anemia.
    b. chronic inflammation.
    c. osteoporosis.
    d. stroke.

15. A diet high in saturated and *trans* fat and cholesterol most increases the likelihood of developing:
    a. cancer.
    b. heart disease.
    c. hypertension.
    d. osteoporosis.

16. Excessive alcohol intake contributes to the development of all of the following EXCEPT:
    a. heart disease.
    b. cancer.
    c. stroke.
    d. hypertension.

17. An example of a nutrient-gene interaction is:
    a. cancer promoters being deactivated by a high intake of cabbage and broccoli.
    b. red wine decreasing heart disease risk.
    c. high fiber intake preventing colon cancer.
    d. vitamin C aiding in the absorption of iron.

18. All of the following are characteristics of a stroke EXCEPT:
    a. "hardening of the arteries" in the brain.
    b. it is also known as a cerebral vascular accident.
    c. it is easily diagnosed and treated.
    d. it occurs when a blood vessel in the brain ruptures.

19. A public health problem in the United States among women and young children is anemia due to:
    a. low iron intake.
    b. vitamin D deficiency.
    c. high sodium intake.
    d. chronic inflammation.

20. All of the following are true regarding tooth decay EXCEPT:
    a. fluoride helps prevent tooth decay.
    b. "sticky sweets" contribute to gum disease.
    c. high and frequent sugar consumption is related to tooth decay.
    d. sugar-free gum prevents tooth decay.

21. Osteoporosis can be defined as:
    a. degeneration of the liver.
    b. bone fragility due to a loss of calcium and other minerals.
    c. abnormally high levels of blood glucose.
    d. inflammation due to infection.

22. Which of the following countries have the highest life expectancies?
    a. United States and Japan
    b. United States, Switzerland, and Australia
    c. Japan and Switzerland
    d. Japan, Italy, and Canada

23. All of the following are *Healthy People 2010* objectives EXCEPT:
    a. Reduce food allergy deaths, increase food security, and decrease sodium intake.
    b. Reduce overweight, increase breastfeeding, and increase whole grain consumption.
    c. Decrease soda consumption, increase food safety practices, and decrease calcium intake.
    d. Reduce cancer, increase healthy weight gain in pregnancy, and increase fruit intake.

24. All of the following are surveys of diet and health in the United States EXCEPT:
    a. Fast Food Consumption Survey.
    b. National Health and Nutrition Examination Survey.
    c. National Food Consumption Survey.
    d. Total Diet Study.

25. All of the following are factors contributing to the rise in obesity EXCEPT:
    a. modern diets are greatly different from those of our ancestors.
    b. the human body has survival mechanisms for increasing appetite and storing fat.
    c. human beings have an innate preference for sweet-tasting foods.
    d. our genes have changed due to the increase in technology and increased food supply.

26. Environmental exposure refers to which of the following?
    a. Access to healthcare
    b. Presence of toxins and disease-causing organisms in one's surroundings
    c. Number of fast-food restaurants within ten miles of one's house
    d. Availability of fast food in schools

27. Excessive body fat is associated with which of the following?
    a. Gum disease
    b. Diabetes
    c. Osteoporosis
    d. Rickets

28. Chronic inflammation is a risk factor for all of the following EXCEPT:
    a. Alzheimer's disease.
    b. cancer.
    c. heart disease.
    d. sinusitis.

29. The decline in heart disease can be attributed to which of the following?
    a. An increase in fat and cholesterol intake
    b. An increase in soluble fiber intake
    c. A decrease in rates of smoking and an increase in physical activity
    d. A decrease in fat and cholesterol intake and a decrease in rates of smoking

12

30. Chronic inflammation can be BEST described as:
    a. inflammation that lasts for up to a week.
    b. the last response by the body's immune system to infection.
    c. inflammation that triggers the release of substances that promote oxidation.
    d. inflammation which is limited to the arteries.

To check your answers, use the answer key at the bottom of the page.[3]

---

[3] 1. b, 2. c, 3. d, 4. c, 5. b, 6. a, 7. c, 8. d, 9. b, 10. b, 11. c, 12. c, 13. b, 14. a, 15. b, 16. a, 17. a, 18. c, 19. a, 20. d, 21. b, 22. c, 23. c, 24. a, 25. d, 26. b, 27. b, 28. d, 29. d, 30. c

Unit 3 – Ways of Knowing about Nutrition

Key Concepts

- For the most part, nutrition information offered to the public does not have to be true or even likely true.
- Nutrition information offered to the public ranges in quality from sound and beneficial to outrageous and harmful.
- Science is knowledge gained by systematic study. Reliable information about nutrition and health is generated by scientific studies.
- Misleading and fraudulent nutrition information exists primarily because of financial interests and personal beliefs and convictions.

Unit Outline

I. How do I know if what I read or hear about nutrition is true?
   A. Why is there so much nutrition misinformation?
      1. Motivation for nutrition misinformation #1: profit
         a. Controlling profit-motivated nutrition frauds
         b. Science for sale
         c. Who is conducting the research?
         d. A checklist for identifying nutrition misinformation
         e. The business of nutrition news
   B. Motivation for nutrition misinformation #2: personal beliefs and convictions
      1. Professionals with embedded beliefs
II. How to identify nutrition truths
   A. Sources of reliable nutrition information
      1. Nutrition information on the Web
      2. Who are qualified nutrition professionals?
III. The methods of science
   A. Developing the plan
   B. The hypothesis: making the question testable
   C. The research design: gathering the right information
      1. What type of research design should be used?
         a. The experimental and control groups
         b. The "placebo effect"
      2. Who should the research subjects be?
      3. How many subjects are needed in the study?
      4. What information needs to be collected?
      5. What are accurate ways to collect the needed information?
      6. What statistical tests should be used to analyze the findings?
   D. Obtaining approval to study human subjects
   E. Implementing the study
   F. Making sense of the results
      1. Science and personal decisions about nutrition

Unit Glossary

- **Association:** The finding that one condition is correlated with, or related to another condition, such as a disease or disorder. For example, diets low in vegetables are associated with breast cancer. Associations do not prove that one condition (such as a diet low in vegetables) causes an event (such as breast cancer). They indicate that a statistically significant relationship between a condition and an event exists.

- **Cause and effect:** A finding that demonstrates that a condition causes a particular event. For example, vitamin C deficiency causes the deficiency disease scurvy.
- **Clinical trial:** A study design in which one group of randomly assigned subjects (or subjects selected by the "luck of the draw") receives an active treatment and another group receives an inactive treatment, or "sugar pill," called the placebo.
- **Control group:** Subjects in a study who do not receive the active treatment or who do not have the condition under investigation. Control periods, or times when subjects are not receiving the treatment, are sometimes used instead of a control group.
- **Double blind:** A study in which neither the subjects participating in the research nor the scientists performing the research know which subjects are receiving the treatment and which are getting the placebo. Both subjects and investigators are "blind" to the treatment administered.
- **Epidemiological studies:** Research that seeks to identify conditions related to particular events within a population. This type of research does not identify cause-and-effect relationships. For example, much of the information known about diet and cancer is based on epidemiological studies that have found that diets low in vegetables and fruits are associated with the development of heart disease.
- **Experimental group:** Subjects in a study who receive the treatment being tested or have the condition that is being investigated.
- **Hypothesis:** A statement made prior to initiating a study of the relationship sought to be tested by the research.
- **Meta-analysis:** An analysis of data from multiple studies. Results are based on larger samples than the individual studies and are therefore more reliable. Differences in methods and subjects among the studies may bias the results of meta-analyses.
- **Peer review:** Evaluation of the scientific merit of research or scientific reports by experts in the area under review. Studies published in scientific journals have gone through peer review prior to being accepted for publication.
- **Placebo:** A "sugar pill," an imitation treatment given to subjects in research.
- **Placebo effect:** Changes in health or perceived health that result from expectations that a "treatment" will produce an effect on health.
- **Statistically significant:** Research findings that likely represent a true or actual result and not one due to chance.

Practice Multiple-Choice Test

1. Fraudulent nutrition products typically share all of the following characteristics EXCEPT:
    a. they offer customers a money-back guarantee.
    b. they have a scientific-sounding explanation.
    c. they identify a problem that is easily fixed.
    d. they contain a testimonial from an "expert."

2. Nutrition misinformation can be identified by asking all of the following EXCEPT:
    a. Is something being sold?
    b. Does the product sound too good to be true?
    c. Is the product expensive?
    d. Does the product use terms such as "miraculous" and "secret"?

3. Nutrition is in the media spotlight frequently due to all of the following reasons EXCEPT:
   a. there are a large number of nutrition-related articles published monthly.
   b. nutrition breakthroughs increase the number of readers or viewers.
   c. profits increase when the number of readers or viewers increases.
   d. the media is committed to improving the health of its readers or viewers.

4. All of the following are elements of a nutrition research study EXCEPT:
   a. posing an ambiguous question to be answered.
   b. stating the hypothesis to be tested.
   c. deciding on a study design.
   d. evaluating the findings.

5. Which of the following are valid research designs?
   a. Epidemiological and causal
   b. Experiential and factual
   c. Epidemiological and factual
   d. Epidemiological and clinical trial

6. Studies on nutrition use two groups of subjects who are called the:
   a. peer group and control group.
   b. scientific group and control group.
   c. experimental group and control group.
   d. placebo group and control group.

7. Which of the following is an example of the placebo effect?
   a. Experimental bias from the researcher
   b. Subjects who receive the treatment
   c. Expectations influencing the results
   d. Subjects who drop out of the study

8. All of the following are important considerations regarding subjects EXCEPT:
   a. type of subjects.
   b. number of subjects.
   c. prior knowledge about the purpose of the study.
   d. the information that should be collected.

9. Nutrition information in magazines, the Internet, and TV:
   a. is backed by scientific knowledge.
   b. can be trusted as a valid source of information.
   c. is protected by freedom of speech under the U.S. Constitution.
   d. is required to meet standards of truth.

10. It is legal to make false claims on TV and the Internet, but it is illegal to:
    a. put misleading information on a product label.
    b. put misleading information in a tabloid.
    c. promote a product that does not work on the radio.
    d. make false claims in a newspaper article.

11. Nutrition misinformation exists for all of the following reasons EXCEPT:
    a. freedom of speech.
    b. truth in advertising laws are strictly enforced.
    c. profit.
    d. personal beliefs and convictions.

12. People purchase fraudulent nutrition products for all of the following reasons EXCEPT:
    a. they are looking for a "quick fix."
    b. people tend to believe what they see and hear.
    c. health insurance covers the cost.
    d. information is made to sounds scientific and believable.

13. Which of the following agencies has the authority to remove false claims from the airwaves and Internet advertisements?
    a. Food and Drug Administration
    b. Federal Trade Commission
    c. Environmental Protection Agency
    d. United States Drug Administration

14. When a consumer suspects a product has made a false claim, he or she should:
    a. call the police.
    b. file a complaint with the FTC.
    c. complain to the store manager.
    d. file a complaint with the EPA.

15. "Personal beliefs and convictions" refers to:
    a. products sold because they are tested for safety and effectiveness.
    b. the motivation behind remedies sold by alternative health practitioners.
    c. proof of product efficacy.
    d. a desire to fool the public.

16. Sources of reliable nutrition information include all of the following EXCEPT:
    a. registered dietitians.
    b. nonprofit, professional health organizations.
    c. commercial websites.
    d. government publications.

17. All of the following are qualified nutrition professionals EXCEPT:
    a. health store employees.
    b. registered dietitians.
    c. licensed dietitians/nutritionists.
    d. certified dietitians/nutritionists.

18. All of the following organizations are reliable sources of nutrition information EXCEPT:
    a. the United States Dairy Council.
    b. university extension services.
    c. talk show hosts.
    d. the Surgeon General.

19. Which of the following best describes the credentials that a registered dietitian holds?
    a. Minimum B.S. in nutrition, accredited internship, national certification exam
    b. Minimum B.S. in nutrition
    c. Minimum B.S. in health, personal trainer certification
    d. Minimum B.S. in nutrition, training in diet counseling

20. Which of the following is the definition of the scientific method?
    a. Study results generated through opinion polls
    b. Study questions generated as a result of product promotions
    c. A carefully planned process for answering a specific question
    d. Study results generated through chance discoveries

21. A hypothesis can be defined as:
    a. a finding that demonstrates a cause and effect.
    b. a study in which one group is randomly assigned.
    c. a statement made prior to initiating the study to be proved or disproved.
    d. subjects who do not receive the treatment in a study.

22. Study information that should be collected includes which of the following?
    a. Only supportive evidence
    b. Only evidence that disproves the question
    c. Evidence that both supports and refutes the question
    d. Evidence that leaves questions for further study

23. Research designs should answer all of the following questions EXCEPT:
    a. What type of research design should be used?
    b. What are accurate methods for data collection?
    c. What statistical tests should be used to analyze the findings?
    d. Who should fund the study?

24. A double-blind experiment is one in which:
    a. both the scientists and the subjects know who is receiving the treatment.
    b. neither the scientists nor the subjects know who is receiving the treatment.
    c. only the scientists know who is receiving the treatment.
    d. only the human subjects committee and the scientists know who is receiving treatment.

25. A study is statistically significant if which of the following is true?
    a. The findings represent the expected effect.
    b. The findings do not represent the expected effect.
    c. The findings represent a result due to chance.
    d. The findings represent a result that is not due to chance.

26. A finding that demonstrates that a condition produces a particular event is termed:
    a. an association.
    b. statistically significant.
    c. cause and effect.
    d. a clinical trial.

18

27. What committee must grant prior approval to research using human subjects?
    a. Federal Drug Administration
    b. Expert panels of scientists
    c. Food and Drug Administration
    d. Institutional Review Board

28. Which of the following should help you in making nutrition decisions?
    a. Information on the Internet
    b. Scientific evidence
    c. Information you read in a tabloid
    d. Information you hear on TV

29. Which of the following describes a meta-analysis?
    a. An educated guess
    b. Evaluation of scientific reports by peers
    c. An analysis of data from multiple studies
    d. The finding that one condition is correlated with another

30. The most important step of a research study is:
    a. the statistical analysis of the results.
    b. the journal in which the results are published.
    c. the planning process.
    d. the implementation process.

To check yourself, use the answer key at the bottom of the page.[4]

---

[4] 1. c, 2. c, 3. d, 4. a , 5. d, 6. c, 7. c, 8. c, 9. c, 10. a, 11. b, 12. c, 13. b, 14. b, 15. b, 16. c, 17. a, 18. c, 19. a, 20. c, 21. c, 22. c, 23. d, 24. b, 25. d, 26. c, 27. d, 28. b, 29. c, 30. c

Unit 4 – Understanding Food and Nutrition Labels

Key Concepts

- People have a right to know what is in the food they buy.
- The purpose of nutrition labeling is to give people information about the composition of food products so they can make informed food purchasing decisions.
- Nutrition labeling regulations cover the type of foods that must be labeled and set the standards for the content and format of labels.

Unit Outline

I. Nutrition labeling
   A. Key elements of nutrition labeling standards
      1. The Nutrition Facts panel
         a. Daily Values (DVs)
      2. Nutrient content
      3. Health Claims
         a. Labeling foods as enriched or fortified
      4. The ingredient label
      5. Food additives on the label
         a. Irradiated foods
   B. Dietary supplement labeling
      1. Structure/function claims
   C. The COOL Rule
   D. Organic foods
      1. Labeling organic foods
   E. The nutrition labeling transition
      1. The new wave of nutrition labels
      2. Calories on display
II. Beyond nutrition labels: we still need to think

Unit Glossary

- **% Daily Value (%DV):** Daily Values are scientifically agreed-upon standards of daily intake of nutrients from the diet developed for use on nutrition labels. The "% Daily Values" listed in nutrition labels represent the percentages of the standards obtained from one serving of the food product.
- **enrichment:** The replacement of thiamin, riboflavin, niacin, and iron lost when grains are refined.
- **fortification:** The addition of one or more vitamins and/or minerals to a food product.
- **food additives:** Any substances added to food that become part of the food or affect the characteristics of the food. The term applies to substances added both intentionally and unintentionally to food.
- **dietary supplement:** Any product intended to supplement the diet, including vitamins, minerals, proteins, enzymes, herbs, hormones, and organ tissues. Such products must be labeled "Dietary Supplement."
- **structure/function claim:** Statement appearing primarily on dietary supplement labels that describes the effect a supplement may have on the structure or function of the body. Such statements cannot claim to diagnose, cure, mitigate, treat, or prevent disease.

20

Practice Multiple-Choice Test

1. Which of the following best describes labeling laws regarding foods sold in a supermarket deli?
    a. Nutrition information must be displayed as a poster.
    b. A nutrition pamphlet must be provided to the customer for each item.
    c. Nutrition labeling of raw meats and cheeses is strictly voluntary.
    d. Nutrition information is stamped on the paper used for wrapping the purchase.

2. All of the following are required to be listed on the Nutrition Facts panel EXCEPT:
    a. total calories.
    b. % Daily Values.
    c. monounsaturated fat.
    d. *trans* fat.

3. Which two vitamins are required to be listed on the Nutrition Facts panel?
    a. Vitamin A and vitamin K
    b. Vitamin B_{12} and vitamin D
    c. Folate and riboflavin
    d. Vitamin A and vitamin C

4. Which two minerals are required to be listed on the Nutrition Facts panel?
    a. Zinc and iron
    b. Vitamin B_{12} and vitamin D
    c. Calcium and iron
    d. Vitamin A and vitamin K

5. All of the following are examples of FDA-approved nutrient claims EXCEPT:
    a. "high fiber" to refer to a food with 30% of the DV for fiber.
    b. "improves circulation" if the food has 140 milligrams or less of sodium.
    c. "fat free" if the food has less than 0.5 grams of fat.
    d. "good source" if the food has 20% or more of the DV for a particular nutrient.

6. All of the following are true regarding nutrient claims EXCEPT:
    a. they can be used to make a food appear healthier for you.
    b. they must conform to standard definitions.
    c. they are subject to FDA approval.
    d. they must be truthful.

7. Which of the following best describes *enrichment*?
    a. The replacement of thiamin, fiber, and iron lost when grains are refined
    b. The addition of one or more vitamins and/or minerals to a food product
    c. The replacement of thiamin, riboflavin, niacin, and iron lost when grains are refined
    d. The addition of vitamins, minerals, and protein to a food product

8. Which of the following best describes *fortification*?
    a. The replacement of thiamin, fiber, and iron lost when grains are refined
    b. The addition of one or more vitamins and/or minerals to a food product
    c. The replacement of thiamin, riboflavin, niacin, and iron lost when grains are refined
    d. The addition of vitamins, minerals, and protein to a food product

9. Which of the following is the term for the international symbol for irradiated foods?
    a. GRAS
    b. Radura
    c. "Big Green"
    d. %DV

10. Foods certified as organic by the FDA:
    a. can carry a green "radura" symbol.
    b. use only small amounts of pesticides.
    c. must carry the words "grown organically."
    d. can carry a green-and-white USDA Organic seal.

11. All of the following foods are required by law to have a Nutrition Facts label EXCEPT:
    a. items on a restaurant menu.
    b. a jar of salsa.
    c. a bag of salad greens.
    d. a box of cereal.

12. Which of the following acts passed by Congress pertains to nutrition labeling?
    a. 1990 Truth in Advertising Act
    b. 1993 Consumer Information Act
    c. 1990 Nutrition Labeling and Education Act
    d. 1990 Food and Drug Administration Nutrient Density Act

13. Which of the following federal agencies publishes rules and revisions for nutrition labeling?
    a. EPA
    b. FDA
    c. USDA
    d. FERPA

14. Which of the following is NOT required to carry nutrition information?
    a. An item sold in a can
    b. A carton of egg substitute
    c. A container of yogurt
    d. An item sold at a bakery

15. Which of the following BEST describes the % Daily Value?
    a. It refers to the % of the product that is a reasonable portion size.
    b. It refers to the reference material for calculating the percentage of calories from fat.
    c. It is the percentage of the recommended daily amounts provided by one serving of the food.
    d. It is important to note if you do not consume 2500 calories per day.

16. All of the following are true regarding the serving sizes on nutrition labels EXCEPT:
    a. they represent portion sizes that are reasonable and generally consumed.
    b. they are standard serving sizes developed by the FDA.
    c. a serving of fruit juice will be 6 ounces regardless of brand.
    d. the manufacturer determines the serving size.

17. Which of the following is a voluntary component of the Nutrition Facts panel?
    a. Calories from saturated fat
    b. Dietary fiber
    c. Vitamin A
    d. Sugars

18. Daily Values have not been assigned for which of the following?
    a. Calories from fat
    b. Cholesterol
    c. Sodium
    d. *Trans* fat

19. Which information on the Nutrition Facts panel is intended to help the consumer choose the most nutritious brand of a particular food?
    a. Serving size
    b. % Daily Value
    c. % RDA
    d. Ingredient list

20. All of the following are true regarding % Daily Values EXCEPT:
    a. they are based on earlier editions of the RDAs.
    b. they are standard levels of daily nutrient intakes developed just for food labels.
    c. standard values for total fat and carbohydrate are based on a 2000-calorie diet.
    d. the % DV for total fat is based on 35% of total calories from fat.

21. Which of the following CANNOT be labeled with a nutrition claim?
    a. A food that is high in sodium, sugar, and cholesterol
    b. A food that is high in calcium and fiber
    c. A food that is low in sodium, sugar, and cholesterol
    d. A food that is high in calcium, vitamin C, and fiber

22. Which of the following is NOT an approved health claim for food and disease prevention?
    a. Whole grains and heart disease
    b. Folic acid and neural tube defects
    c. Calcium and osteoporosis
    d. Calcium and arthritis

23. All of the following are reasons that people choose organic foods EXCEPT:
    a. they do not contain pesticides.
    b. they do not contain hormones.
    c. they have a longer shelf life.
    d. they are grown according to strict USDA regulations.

24. All of the following describes a health claim EXCEPT:
    a. the food must have scientifically agreed-upon benefits to disease prevention to carry a claim.
    b. claims are based on FDA "model claim" statements.
    c. claims are based on foods and related health issues.
    d. claims are based on prevention of deficiency diseases such as rickets.

25. Ingredients on a food label are listed:
    a. in ascending order by weight.
    b. alphabetically.
    c. in descending order by weight.
    d. in descending order by calorie content.

26. All of the following are true regarding food additives EXCEPT:
    a. they may be either intentional or unintentional additives.
    b. the most common additives are sugar and salt.
    c. the term *food additive* refers to any substance added to food that becomes part of the food.
    d. unintentional additives include potassium benzoate and xanthan gum.

27. All of the following are true regarding dietary supplements EXCEPT:
    a. they are required by the FDA to undergo safety testing before they are sold.
    b. this term refers to a product taken by mouth and intended to supplement the diet.
    c. they are required by the FDA to carry a "Supplements Facts" panel.
    d. they can include vitamins, proteins, minerals, enzymes, herbs, and organ tissues.

28. All of the following are true regarding structure/function claims EXCEPT:
    a. they often appear on dietary supplement labels.
    b. they can claim to diagnose, cure, treat, or prevent a disease.
    c. they can include statements such as " helps maintain mental health."
    d. they must acknowledge that the FDA does not support the claim.

29. All of the following are true regarding irradiated foods EXCEPT:
    a. they must display the words "treated by irradiation."
    b. they generally have a longer shelf life.
    c. they are safe to eat.
    d. they contain minute amounts of radioactive materials.

30. Plants grown organically:
    a. can be fertilized with sewer sludge.
    b. can use genetically modified ingredients.
    c. cannot be grown in soil treated with synthetic fertilizers 5 years previously.
    d. cannot be grown in soil treated with pesticides within the past 3 years.

To check yourself, use the answer key at the bottom of the page.[5]

---

[5] 1. c, 2. c, 3. d, 4. c, 5. b, 6. a, 7. c, 8. b, 9. b, 10. d, 11. a, 12. c, 13. b, 14. d, 15. c, 16. d, 17. a, 18. d, 19. b, 20. d, 21. a, 22. d, 23. c, 24. d, 25. c, 26. d, 27. a, 28. b, 29. d, 30. d

Unit 5 – Nutrition, Attitudes, and Behavior

Key Concepts

- Most food preferences are learned.
- The value a person assigns to eating right has more effect on dietary behaviors than does knowledge about how to eat right.
- Food habits can and do change.
- The smaller and more acceptable the dietary change, the longer it lasts.
- Behavior and mental performance can be affected by diet.

Unit Outline

I. Origins of food choices
    A. We don't instinctively know what to eat
II. Food choices and preferences
    A. The symbolic meaning of food
        1. Status foods
        2. Comfort foods
        3. "Discomfort foods"
    B. Cultural values surrounding food
    C. Other factors influencing food choices and preferences
        1. Food cost and availability
        2. Genetic influences
III. Food choices do change
    A. How do food choices change?
        1. Nutrition knowledge and food choices
        2. When knowledge isn't enough
        3. Nutrition attitudes, beliefs, and values
    B. Successful changes in food choices
        1. The process of changing food choices
        2. Planning for relapses
IV. Does diet affect behavior?
    A. Malnutrition and mental performance
        1. Does breakfast help you think better?
        2. Early exposure to alcohol affects mental performance
        3. Iron deficiency impairs learning
        4. Overexposure to lead
        5. Food additives, sugar, and hyperactivity
    B. The future of diet and behavior research

Practice Multiple-Choice Test

1. Which if the following is NOT an example of cultural influences on food selection?
    a. Heredity
    b. Customs
    c. Food symbolism
    d. Religious beliefs

2. Factors influencing food selection and dietary quality include all of the following EXCEPT:
   a. culture.
   b. food preferences.
   c. practical considerations.
   d. food selection genes.

3. Which of the following describes the role that genetics plays in food preference development?
   a. Some people are born with a preference for fruits and vegetables.
   b. Most people are born with a preference for chocolate.
   c. Some people are born with a sensitivity to bitterness.
   d. Some people are born with a preference for red meat.

4. All of the following are true regarding comfort foods EXCEPT:
   a. the most common ones in the U.S. are ice cream, apple pie, and chicken soup.
   b. they are foods with symbolic value.
   c. they are foods associated with pleasant memories.
   d. they are foods associated with unpleasant memories.

5. Since 1990, all of the following are changes that occurred in American's food choices EXCEPT:
   a. sugar consumption has increased by 17%.
   b. chicken consumption has increased by 33%.
   c. whole milk consumption has increased by 25%.
   d. margarine consumption has decreased by 42%.

6. How does nutrition knowledge influence food choices?
   a. It is all that most people need to make healthful changes
   b. It motivates some, but not all, people to make healthful changes
   c. It provides the greatest motivation to change for "unconcerned" consumers
   d. It rarely helps "committed" consumers to make healthful changes

7. Which of the following groups of people is most likely to be successful in making positive dietary changes?
   a. "Committed" consumers
   b. "Vacillating" consumers
   c. "Unconcerned" consumers
   d. "Pre-contemplation" consumers

8. All of the following are effects of severe protein-calorie deficiency early in life EXCEPT:
   a. increased intelligence.
   b. social passivity.
   c. growth retardation.
   d. poor memory.

9. Overexposure to lead in children can produce which of the following effects?
   a. Impaired reading skills and long-term behavioral effects
   b. Hyperactivity
   c. Iron toxicity
   d. Criminal behavior

26

10. All of the following are unsubstantiated claims about diet and behavior EXCEPT:
    a. food colorant intakes are related to hyperactivity in children.
    b. vitamin/mineral supplementation is related to increased intelligence in healthy children.
    c. breakfast consumption is related to overweight in children.
    d. sugar intake is related to hyperactivity in children.

11. *Food preferences* refers most directly to which of the following?
    a. Cost and convenience
    b. Taste, familiarity, and heredity
    c. Customs
    d. Attitudes and values

12. The factor that has the largest influence on food choices for most people is:
    a. culture.
    b. level of hunger.
    c. food preference.
    d. education.

13. Humans are born with mechanisms that:
    a. help them to resist high-calorie foods if they are overweight.
    b. guide pregnant women to instinctively choose a good diet.
    c. seek out food rich in iron if they are deficient in iron.
    d. help them decide when and how much to eat.

14. An example of cultivating a preference for a status food would be:
    a. preferring steak if you could only afford beans as a child.
    b. an inborn preference for sweets that makes you seek cookies as an adult.
    c. a need to demonstrate superior intelligence.
    d. avoiding foods that run contrary to your values and beliefs.

15. Americans are exposed to approximately _____ new food items in grocery stores each year.
    a. 100,000
    b. 200-500
    c. 2000
    d. 20,000

16. Which of the following is an established relationship between diet and behavior?
    a. Sugar intake, hyperactivity, and criminal behavior
    b. Meat and aggressive behavior
    c. Autism and food allergies
    d. Breakfast-skipping and reduced problem-solving skills in children

17. Practical considerations influencing foods choices include all of the following EXCEPT:
    a. food cost.
    b. attitudes and values.
    c. convenience.
    d. food availability.

18. An example of food availability affecting food choices would be:
    a. the desire to consume foods that are considered healthy.
    b. selecting more low-fat and high-fiber foods when presented with a wide selection.
    c. modifying cultural norms for food acceptance.
    d. seeking status foods.

19. All of the following are true regarding food choices EXCEPT:
    a. they are largely learned.
    b. they can change as our nutrition knowledge increases.
    c. they are driven by our genetic makeup.
    d. they can change as our attitudes towards food selection change.

20. Successful dietary changes are most likely a combination of all of the following EXCEPT:
    a. the value placed on diet and health.
    b. putting knowledge into practice.
    c. seeing that the benefits of making the changes outweigh the disadvantages.
    d. trying to make as many major changes as possible at the same time.

21. All of the following are factors that enhance food changes EXCEPT:
    a. perceived susceptibility to diet-related health problems.
    b. a belief that diet affects health.
    c. subscribing to a health magazine.
    d. an attitude that nutrition is important.

22. Attempted changes in food choices succeed when:
    a. you eliminate all high-fat foods and sugars at once.
    b. you eliminate all restaurant dining.
    c. you decide to just "eat less."
    d. you identify one or two changes that would be easiest to implement.

23. All of the following are established relationships between diet and behavior EXCEPT:
    a. iron-deficiency anemia is related to reduced attention span.
    b. sugar intake is related to over-activity and impulsiveness.
    c. severe protein-calorie malnutrition early in life is related to impaired mental development.
    d. overexposure to lead is related to poor academic performance.

24. Which of the following is true regarding fetal exposure to alcohol?
    a. Fetal exposure to alcohol can result in permanent delays in mental development.
    b. Pregnant women are advised to consume only 2-3 alcoholic drinks per week.
    c. Growth retardation is the most serious effect of fetal exposure to alcohol.
    d. Intense treatment can reverse the mental and behavioral effects of fetal exposure to alcohol.

25. Which of the following is NOT believed to be an inborn food intake regulation mechanism in humans?
    a. Increased thirst response during periods of dehydration
    b. Decreased hunger when the stomach is full and distended
    c. Decreased preference for bitter foods in response to iron deficiency
    d. Increased preference for salty foods in response to sodium deficiency

28

26. Which of the following is the most common single nutrient deficiency in children?
    a. Vitamin D deficiency
    b. Iron deficiency
    c. Vitamin C deficiency
    d. Calcium deficiency

27. Why is the effect of diet on behavior difficult to study?
    a. There is little interest in these effects among the public
    b. Subjects' food intakes are difficult to analyze
    c. Many factors in addition to diet influence behavior
    d. Diet cannot influence behavior

28. Which of the following has the best scientific evidence supporting the claim?
    a. Very-low-carbohydrate diets can reduce short-term memory.
    b. Low-carbohydrate diets reduce fat intake.
    c. High-carbohydrate meals decrease appetite.
    d. High-carbohydrate diets increase LDL cholesterol production.

29. Which of the following is true regarding sugar intake?
    a. It increases hyperactivity in children.
    b. It is linked to increased criminal behavior.
    c. Intake of sugars and carbohydrates may increase activity level in children and adults.
    d. It has not been demonstrated to increase hyperactivity in children.

30. Which of the following is true regarding the effects of nutrition on behavior?
    a. The research is complete.
    b. It is quite easy to separate dietary from social and economic influences.
    c. The research is incomplete.
    d. It is impossible to study objectively.

To check yourself, use the answer key at the bottom of the page.[6]

---

[6] 1. a, 2. d, 3. c, 4. d, 5. c, 6. b, 7. a, 8. a, 9. a, 10. a, 11. b, 12. c, 13. d, 14. a, 15. d, 16. d, 17. b, 18. b, 19. c, 20. d, 21. c, 22. d, 23. b, 24. a, 25. c, 26. b, 27. c, 28. a, 29. d, 30. c

Unit 6 – Healthy Diets, Dietary Guidelines, MyPyramid, and More

Key Concepts

- Healthful diets are characterized by adequacy and balance.
- There are many types of healthful diets.
- The Dietary Guidelines for Americans and MyPyramid Food Guide provide foundation information for healthful diets and physical activity levels.

Unit Outline

I. Healthy eating: achieving the balance between good taste and good for you
   A. Characteristics of healthful diets
   B. How balanced is the American diet?
II. Guides to healthy diets
III. Dietary Guidelines for Americans
   A. Focus areas and key recommendations
   B. Implementation of the Dietary Guidelines
IV. MyPyramid food guide
   A. What's in MyPyramid?
   B. MyPyramid.gov: the Web site
      1. Limitations of MyPyramid
   C. The DASH Diet
      1. The Mediterranean diet
   D. Portion distortion
      1. Is supersizing leading to supersized Americans?
   E. Can you still eat right when eating out?
      1. Staying on track while eating out
      2. Can fast foods be part of a healthy diet?
   F. The slow food movement
   G. What if you don't know how to cook?
V. Bon appétit!

Unit Glossary

- **adequate diet:** A diet consisting of foods that together supply sufficient protein, vitamins, and minerals and enough calories to meet a person's need for energy.
- **essential nutrients:** Substances the body requires for normal growth and health but cannot manufacture in sufficient amounts; they must be obtained in the diet.
- **balanced diet:** A diet that provides neither too much nor too little of nutrients and other components of food such as fat and fiber.
- **macronutrients:** The group name for the energy-yielding nutrients of carbohydrate, protein, and fat. They are called macronutrients because we need relatively large amounts of them in our daily diet.
- **saturated fats:** The type of fat that tends to raise blood cholesterol levels and the risk for heart disease. They are solid at room temperature and are found primarily in animal products such as meat, butter, and cheese.
- *trans* **fats:** A type of unsaturated fat present in hydrogenated oils, margarine, shortening, pastries, and some cooking oils that increases the risk of heart disease.
- **hypertension:** High blood pressure. It is defined as blood pressure exerted inside blood vessel walls that typically exceeds 140/90 millimeters of mercury.

Practice Multiple-Choice Test

1. All of the following describe macronutrients EXCEPT:
   a. they are energy yielding.
   b. they include proteins, carbohydrates, and fats.
   c. they are needed in relatively small amounts.
   d. guidelines for recommended intake are known as the "AMDRs."

2. A tool that is available to assist consumers in implementing the 2005 Dietary Guidelines is:
   a. the Basic Four Food Groups.
   b. the Food Guide Pyramid.
   c. MyPyramid.
   d. the New American Plate.

3. Which online tool is NOT correctly matched with its function?
   a. "MyPyramid Menu Planner" – allows you to develop your own menus based on calorie need
   b. "MyPyramid Plan" – provides explanations about each food group and discretionary calories
   c. "MyPyramid for Kids" – provides games and resources for elementary school-age children
   d. "For Professionals" – provides 7 days of sample menus for a 2000-calorie pattern

4. Limitations of MyPyramid include all of the following EXCEPT:
   a. it does not provide specific recommendations for pregnant or breastfeeding women.
   b. there are no recommendations for strict vegetarians.
   c. materials are almost entirely available on the Web.
   d. menus offered on MyPyramid contain relatively few ethnic foods.

5. All of the following are true regarding the DASH diet EXCEPT:
   a. it helps to control mild and moderate high blood pressure.
   b. it emphasizes fruits, vegetables, low-fat dairy foods, lean protein, and nuts.
   c. it stands for Daily Approaches to Stop Hyperglycemia.
   d. the diet provides ample amounts of potassium, magnesium, and calcium.

6. All of the following are true regarding the Mediterranean diet EXCEPT:
   a. it is associated with a reduced rate of heart disease.
   b. it is associated with a reduced rate of overall mortality.
   c. it is high in fruits, vegetables, and olive oil.
   d. it includes red meat in moderate portions weekly.

7. All of the following are true regarding portion sizes EXCEPT:
   a. a portion size is the same as a standard serving size.
   b. portion sizes have increased in the last several years.
   c. supersizing fast foods can double or triple their caloric content.
   d. it is suspected that the rising rates of obesity are due to increases in portion sizes.

8. All of the following are true regarding the typical U.S. diet EXCEPT:
   a. it is high in added sugars.
   b. it is low in dairy products.
   c. it is low in fruits and vegetables.
   d. it is high in essential fatty acids.

9. All of the following are ways to stick to a healthy diet when eating out EXCEPT:
    a. deciding what you eat before you enter the restaurant.
    b. choosing a smaller portion.
    c. ordering dessert first.
    d. choosing a salad with low-fat dressing instead of a meat entrée.

10. All of the following describe the "Slow Food Movement" EXCEPT:
    a. it is part of an international group.
    b. it supports the use of pesticides to increase crop production.
    c. it supports the revival of the kitchen and table as places of pleasure and community.
    d. it supports a slower and more harmonious rhythm of life.

11. Healthful diets share two main characteristics, including:
    a. completeness and adequacy.
    b. balance and wholesomeness.
    c. low in calories and low in fat.
    d. adequacy and balance.

12. A diet consisting of foods that together supply sufficient protein, vitamins, minerals, and calories to meet a person's need for energy is:
    a. adequate.
    b. balanced.
    c. proportional.
    d. reasonable.

13. A diet that provides neither too much nor too little of nutrients and other components of food such as fat and fiber is:
    a. adequate.
    b. balanced.
    c. sufficient.
    d. ample.

14. The Acceptable Macronutrient Distribution Range for carbohydrates is:
    a. 5-10%.
    b. 20-35%.
    c. 45-65%.
    d. 10-35%.

15. The Acceptable Macronutrient Distribution Range for fat is:
    a. 45-65%.
    b. no more than 25%.
    c. 10-35%.
    d. 20-35%.

16. The Acceptable Macronutrient Distribution Range for protein is:
    a. no more than 25%.
    b. 45-65%.
    c. 10-35%.
    d. 20-35%.

17. Which of the following does NOT raise blood cholesterol level and the risk for heart disease?
    a. *Trans* fats
    b. Saturated fats
    c. Solid fats
    d. Proteins

18. Substances that the body requires for normal growth and health but cannot manufacture in sufficient amounts, and that therefore must be obtained in the diet, are called:
    a. important nutrients.
    b. essential nutrients.
    c. critical nutrients.
    d. nonessential nutrients.

19. The type of fat that tends to raise blood cholesterol levels and risk for heart disease is:
    a. saturated fats.
    b. monounsaturated fats.
    c. polyunsaturated fats.
    d. omega-6 fats.

20. All of the following are true regarding the Dietary Guidelines for Americans EXCEPT:
    a. they are updated every ten years.
    b. they include 23 key recommendations divided into 9 focus areas.
    c. the 2005 edition stresses the importance of selecting nutrient-dense foods.
    d. they are science-based.

21. "Focus Areas" of the 2005 edition of the Dietary Guidelines for Americans include all of the following EXCEPT:
    a. balance calories from food and beverages with calories expended.
    b. consume less than 4,000 mg of sodium per day.
    c. keep *trans* fatty acid consumption as low as possible.
    d. consume 3 cups per day of fat-free or low-fat milk products.

22. All of the following are true regarding *trans* fats EXCEPT:
    a. dietary recommendations are to limit consumption to no more than 10% of total calories.
    b. they are a result of the hydrogenation process.
    c. they are known to increase risk for heart disease.
    d. they are a type of unsaturated fat present in shortening, pastries, and hydrogenated oils.

23. Which is the best example of a healthful dietary variety?
    a. Eating enough food to meet energy needs each day
    b. Drinking orange juice some days and lemonade other days
    c. Eating whole-grain bread each day
    d. Eating a casserole made of 5 differently-colored vegetables

24. Another term for high blood pressure is:
    a. atherosclerosis.
    b. hypertension.
    c. hypoglycemia.
    d. hypotension.

25. All of the following are MyPyramid food measure equivalents EXCEPT:
    a. 2 cups of leafy vegetables equals a 1-cup equivalent.
    b. 1 small egg equals a 2-ounce equivalent.
    c. 1 cup of yogurt equals a 1-cup equivalent.
    d. 1 small apple equals a 1-cup equivalent.

26. All of the following are true regarding meals eaten in restaurants EXCEPT:
    a. they are generally higher in calories than meals served at home.
    b. it is impossible to find any healthy items when dining out.
    c. portions are generally larger than portions eaten at home.
    d. they are generally lower in nutrient content and higher in fat than meals eaten at home.

27. Which of the following recommendations can be used to determine sufficient intake levels of essential nutrients?
    a. AMDRs
    b. RDAs and AIs
    c. EARs
    d. EERs

28. Foods groups that are encouraged in the 2005 Dietary Guidelines include all of the following EXCEPT:
    a. whole-grain products.
    b. fat-free or low-fat dairy products.
    c. *trans* fat.
    d. vegetables from all five subgroups.

29. Recommendations for physical activity include all of the following EXCEPT:
    a. Engage in activity to promote psychological well-being.
    b. Engage in at least 30 minutes of moderate activity 2 to 3 days of the week.
    c. To manage body weight, engage in 60 minutes of moderate to vigorous activity most days.
    d. Engage in physical activity to promote health.

30. Sodium and potassium recommendations include all of the following EXCEPT:
    a. choose and prepare food with little salt.
    b. consume potassium-rich foods such as fruits and vegetables.
    c. consume less than 2,300 mg of sodium per day.
    d. eliminate all processed foods.

To check yourself, use the answer key at the bottom of the page.[7]

------

[7] 1. c, 2. c, 3. b, 4. a, 5. c, 6. d, 7. a, 8. d, 9. c, 10. b, 11. d, 12. a, 13. b, 14. c, 15. d, 16. c, 17. d, 18. b, 19. a, 20. a, 21. b, 22. a, 23. d, 24. b, 25. b, 26. b, 27. b, 28. c, 29. b, 30. d

Unit 7 – How the Body Uses Food: Digestion and Absorption

Key Concepts

- Our bodies are in a continuous state of renewal.
- Materials used to renew body tissues come from the food we eat in the form of nutrients.
- Digestion and absorption are processes that make nutrients in foods available for use by the body.
- Digestive disorders are common and often related to dietary intake.

Unit Outline

I. My body, my food
   A. How do nutrients in food become available for the body's use?
      1. The internal travels of food: an overview
      2. A closer look
      3. Absorption
         a. Beyond absorption
         b. Digestion and absorption are efficient
   B. Digestive disorders are common
      1. Constipation
      2. Myths related to constipation
      3. Ulcers
      4. Heartburn
      5. Irritable bowel syndrome
      6. Diarrhea
      7. Flatulence
      8. Stomach growling
   C. Lactose maldigestion and intolerance
      1. Do you have lactose maldigestion?
      2. How is lactose maldigestion managed?

Unit Glossary

- **digestion:** The mechanical and chemical processes whereby ingested food is converted into substances that can be absorbed by the intestinal tract and utilized by the body.
- **absorption:** The process by which nutrients and other substances are transferred from the digestive system into body fluids for transport throughout the body.
- **monosaccharides** (mono = one, saccharide = sugar): Simple sugars consisting of one sugar molecule. Glucose, fructose, and galactose are monosaccharides.
- **enzymes:** Protein substances that speed up chemical reactions. Enzymes are found throughout the body but are present in particularly large amounts in the digestive system.
- **starch:** Complex carbohydrates made up of complex chains of glucose molecules. Starch is the primary storage form of carbohydrate in plants. The vast majority of carbohydrate in our diet consists of starch, monosaccharides, and disaccharides.
- **disaccharide:** Simple sugars consisting of two sugar molecules. Sucrose (table sugar) consists of a glucose and a fructose molecule, lactose (milk sugar) consists of glucose and galactose, and maltose (malt sugar) consists of two glucose molecules.
- **bile:** A yellowish-brown or green fluid produced by the liver, stored in the gallbladder, and secreted into the small intestine. It acts like a detergent, breaking down globs of fat entering the small intestine to droplets, making the fats more accessible to the action of lipase.

- **lymphatic system:** A network of vessels that absorb some of the products of digestion and transport them to the heart, where they are mixed with the substances contained in blood.
- **circulatory system:** The heart, arteries, capillaries, and veins responsible for circulating blood throughout the body.
- **heartburn:** A condition that results when acidic stomach contents are released into the esophagus, usually causing a burning sensation.
- **hemorrhoids** (hem-or-oids): Swelling of veins in the anus or rectum.
- **irritable bowel syndrome (IBS):** A disorder of bowel function characterized by chronic or episodic gas; abdominal pain; and diarrhea, constipation, or both.
- **duodenal** (do-odd-en-all) and **stomach ulcers:** Open sores in the lining of the duodenum (the uppermost part of the small intestine) or the stomach.
- **probiotics:** Nonharmful bacteria and some yeasts that help colonize the intestinal tract with beneficial microorganisms and that sometimes replace colonies of harmful microorganisms. The most common probiotic strains are *Lactobacilli* and *Bifidobacteria*.
- **diarrhea:** The presence of three or more liquid stools in a 24-hour period.
- **lactose maldigestion:** A disorder characterized by reduced digestion of lactose due to the low availability of the enzyme lactase.
- **lactose intolerance:** The term for gastrointestinal symptoms (flatulence, bloating, abdominal pain, diarrhea, and "rumbling in the bowel") resulting from the consumption of more lactose than can be digested with available lactase.

Practice Multiple-Choice Test

1. Which of the following is a function of the tongue during digestion?
    a. Transfers food to the stomach
    b. Produces enzymes that help break down fats and starch
    c. Mastication and mixing of food with saliva
    d. Prevents food from going into the pharynx during a swallow

2. The surface area of the small intestine is greatly increased by fingerlike projections called:
    a. probiotics.
    b. villi.
    c. diverticula.
    d. mucosa.

3. All of the following describe the lymphatic system EXCEPT:
    a. breakdown products of fat digestion are absorbed here.
    b. breakdown products of proteins and carbohydrates are absorbed here.
    c. nutrients enter the bloodstream from the lymph near the heart.
    d. it includes lymph vessels and lymph nodes.

4. All of the following describe the circulatory system EXCEPT:
    a. breakdown products of fat digestion are absorbed into it from the intestine.
    b. breakdown products of proteins and carbohydrates are absorbed into it from the intestine.
    c. it includes the heart, arteries, capillaries, and veins.
    d. it connects to the lymphatic system and receives lymph from it.

36

5. Absorption can best be defined as the:
   a. transfer of nutrients from the digestive system into all body tissues.
   b. release of energy from chemical substances that are found within foods.
   c. mechanical and chemical breakdown of foods into absorbable units.
   d. transfer of nutrients from the digestive system into the lymphatic/circulatory systems.

6. Which of the following meals would pass through the digestive system fastest?
   a. Low-fiber meals
   b. High-fat meals
   c. Low-fiber, high-fat meals
   d. High-fiber meals

7. The leading causes of hospitalization among U.S. adults 20-44 years old are:
   a. lactose intolerance and milk allergies.
   b. heart disease and cancer.
   c. childbirth and digestive disorders.
   d. digestive disorders and heart disease.

8. Which of the following population groups has the highest incidence of lactose maldigestion?
   a. American Caucasians
   b. Asians
   c. Asian Americans
   d. Africans

9. What is the term for the gastrointestinal symptoms resulting from consuming more lactose than can be digested with available lactase?
   a. Lactose intolerance
   b. Lactose maldigestion
   c. Milk allergy
   d. Irritable bowl syndrome

10. Which of the following best describes the process of digestion?
    a. The transfer of nutrients into the circulatory system
    b. The mechanical and chemical breakdown of foods into absorbable units
    c. Complex proteins that speed up chemical reactions
    d. Production of a yellow-ish brown fluid by the liver

11. Which of the following is NOT a monosaccharide?
    a. Glucose
    b. Galactose
    c. Fructose
    d. Sucrose

12. In order to be absorbed in the body, carbohydrates must be broken down into:
    a. triglycerides.
    b. amino acids.
    c. monosaccharides.
    d. starch.

13. In order to be absorbed in the body, proteins must be broken down into:
    a. triglycerides.
    b. amino acids.
    c. monosaccharides.
    d. starch.

14. In order to be absorbed in the body, fats must be broken down into:
    a. fatty acids and triglycerides.
    b. glucose and fatty acids.
    c. saturated fats.
    d. fatty acids and glycerol.

15. The carbohydrate in our diet consists of all of the following EXCEPT:
    a. amino acids.
    b. starch.
    c. disaccharides.
    d. monosaccharides.

16. Which of the following best describes the characteristics of enzymes?
    a. Protein substances that speed up chemical reactions that break down food
    b. Protein substances that act as chemical messengers to signal when to stop eating
    c. Produced in the kidneys, stomach, and brain
    d. Usable only once before they must be replaced

17. All of the following describe the characteristics of bile EXCEPT:
    a. it separates maltase into two molecules of glucose.
    b. it is produced by the liver and stored in the gallbladder.
    c. it breaks down fats to aid in their digestion.
    d. it enhances the action of lipase.

18. Most nutrient absorption occurs in:
    a. the large intestine.
    b. the small intestine.
    c. the stomach.
    d. the liver.

19. Digestion of carbohydrates begins in the _____ and finishes in the _____.
    a. stomach, large intestine
    b. mouth, small intestine
    c. mouth, large intestine
    d. stomach, small intestine

20. Which of the following nutrients stays in the stomach for the longest amount of time?
    a. Fat
    b. Protein
    c. Carbohydrate
    d. Fiber

©2011 Cengage Learning. All Rights Reserved. May not be scanned, copied or duplicated, or posted to a publicly accessible website, in whole or in part.

38

21. What process occurs in the large intestine?
    a. Fiber binds fatty acids
    b. Pancreatic amylase finishes carbohydrate digestion
    c. Water and sodium are absorbed
    d. Acids complete the breakdown of protein strands

22. Which of the following nutrients passes through the digestive system largely undigested?
    a. Fats
    b. Fiber
    c. Proteins
    d. Triglycerides

23. Which of the following nutrients must be broken down into their single units to be absorbed?
    a. Vitamins
    b. Minerals
    c. Proteins
    d. Water

24. All of the following describe how cells use nutrients EXCEPT:
    a. directly for energy.
    b. for body structures and the regulation of body processes.
    c. as a storage form of energy for later use.
    d. to regulate food intake.

25. Which of the following best describes the efficiency of the digestive system?
    a. 99% of carbohydrates, 92% of proteins, 95% of fats, and no fiber are absorbed
    b. 99% of carbohydrates, 50% of proteins, 95% of fats, and very little fiber are absorbed
    c. 99% of carbohydrates, 92% of proteins, 95% of fats, and most of the fiber are absorbed
    d. 75% of carbohydrates, 50% of proteins, 50% of fats, and very little fiber are absorbed

26. Which of the following digestive disorders is most likely the result of a low-fiber diet?
    a. Lactose intolerance
    b. Heartburn
    c. Hemorrhoids
    d. Ulcers

27. A disorder of bowl function characterized by chronic episodic gas, constipation, and diarrhea is:
    a. an ulcer.
    b. heartburn.
    c. *Helicobacter pylori* syndrome.
    d. irritable bowl syndrome.

28. Duodenal ulcers are closely associated with which of the following?
    a. Drinking too much coffee
    b. Infection from *Helicobacter pylori* bacteria
    c. A low-fiber diet
    d. Infection from *Acidophilus* bacteria

29. Which of the following best describes the function of probiotics?
    a. Nonharmful bacteria that help colonize the intestinal tract
    b. Harmful bacteria that are present in large amounts in protein foods
    c. Bacterial strains such as *Lactobacilli* and *Bifidobacteria* that cause heartburn
    d. Complex carbohydrates added to certain yogurts to benefit the colon

30. A disorder characterized by reduced digestion of lactose due to low lactase enzyme levels is:
    a. lactose intolerance.
    b. lactose maldigestion.
    c. milk allergy.
    d. irritable bowl syndrome.

To check yourself, use the answer key at the bottom of the page.[8]

---

[8] 1. c, 2. b, 3. b, 4. a, 5. d, 6. d, 7. c, 8. c, 9. a, 10. b, 11. d, 12. c, 13. b, 14. d, 15. a, 16. a, 17. a, 18. b, 19. b, 20. a, 21. c, 22. b, 23. c, 24. d, 25. a, 26. c, 27. d, 28. b, 29. a, 30. b

Unit 8 – Calories! Food, Energy, and Energy Balance

Key Concepts

- A calorie is a unit of measure of energy.
- The body's sources of energy are carbohydrates, proteins, and fats (the "energy nutrients").
- Fats provide over twice as many calories per unit weight as carbohydrates and proteins do.
- Most foods contain a mixture of the energy nutrients as well as other substances.
- Weight is gained when caloric intake exceeds the body's need for energy. Weight is lost when caloric intake is less than the body's need for energy.

Unit Outline

I. Energy!
    A. Calories are a unit of measure
    B. The body's need for energy
       1. How much energy do I expend for basal metabolism?
       2. How much energy do I expend in physical activity?
          a. A common source of error
       3. How many calories does dietary thermogenesis take?
       4. Adding it all up
II. Where's the energy in foods?
    A. Most foods are a mixture
III. The caloric value of foods: how do you know?
    A. Energy density
       1. Small differences in energy density make a big difference
    B. How is caloric intake regulated by the body?
       1. The question of energy balance
    C. Keep calories in perspective

Unit Glossary

- **calorie** (calor = heat): A unit of measure used to express the amount of energy produced by foods in the form of heat. The calorie used in nutrition is the large "Calorie," or the "kilocalorie" (kcal). It equals the amount of energy needed to raise the temperature of 1 kilogram of water (about 4 cups) from 15 to 16°C (59 to 61°F). The term kilocalorie, or "calorie" as used in this text, is gradually being replaced by the "kilojoule" (kJ) in the United States; 1 kcal = 4.2 kJ.
- **basal metabolism:** Energy used to support body processes such as growth, health, tissue repair and maintenance, and other functions. Assessed while at rest, basal metabolism includes energy the body expends for breathing, the pumping of the heart, the maintenance of body temperature, and other life-sustaining, ongoing functions.
- **basal metabolic rate (BMR):** The rate at which energy is used by the body when it is at complete rest. BMR is expressed as calories used per unit of time, such as an hour, per unit of body weight in kilograms. Also commonly called resting metabolic rate, or RMR.
- **dietary thermogenesis:** Thermogenesis means "the production of heat." Dietary thermogenesis is the energy expended during the digestion of food and the absorption, utilization, storage, and transport of nutrients. Some of the energy escapes as heat. It accounts for approximately 10% of the body's total energy need. Also called diet-induced thermogenesis and thermic effect of foods or feeding.
- **energy density:** The number of calories in a gram of food. It is calculated by dividing the number of calories in a portion of food by the food's weight in grams.

- **hunger:** Unpleasant physical and psychological sensations (weakness, stomach pains, irritability) that lead people to acquire and ingest food.
- **satiety:** A feeling of fullness or of having had enough to eat.
- **appetite:** The desire to eat; a pleasant sensation that is aroused by thoughts of the taste and enjoyment of food.

Practice Multiple-Choice Test

1. Which of the following statements BEST define a calorie?
   a. A component of food similar to vitamins
   b. A measure of length or weight
   c. A measure of energy
   d. An ingredient added to foods to prolong shelf life

2. An instrument that is used to measure the caloric value of foods is called a(n):
   a. inversion chamber.
   b. bomb calorimeter.
   c. kilojoule.
   d. heat capacitor.

3. All of the following are energy-requiring processes in the body EXCEPT:
   a. satiety.
   b. physical activity.
   c. basal metabolism.
   d. dietary thermogenesis.

4. Which of the following provides no calories?
   a. A candy bar eaten with a diet soda
   b. Celery and grapefruit
   c. Foods tasted while cooking
   d. A calcium supplement taken with water

5. Which of the following nutrients contains the most energy?
   a. Carbohydrate
   b. Fat
   c. Protein
   d. Alcohol

6. The caloric value of a food containing 15 grams of carbohydrate, 10 grams of protein, and 5 grams of fat is:
   a. 120 calories.
   b. 30 calories.
   c. 145 calories.
   d. 60 calories.

7. When energy intake equals energy needs a person is in:
   a. energy balance.
   b. positive energy balance.
   c. negative energy balance.
   d. basal metabolism.

42

8. Positive energy balance is:
   a. when energy intake equals energy needs.
   b. when energy intake is less than energy needs.
   c. the feeling of fullness after eating a big meal.
   d. when energy intake is greater than energy needs.

9. All of the following are true regarding the Calorie EXCEPT:
   a. it is a unit of measure.
   b. it is the amount of energy needed to raise the temperature of 1 kg of water from 15 degrees C to 16 degrees C.
   c. it is a unit of measure used to express the energy released by burned foods in the form of heat.
   d. it is a nonessential nutrient.

10. Which of the following BEST describes basal metabolism?
    a. Energy needed for muscular work
    b. Energy use related to food ingestion
    c. Energy required to maintain normal body functions while at rest
    d. The amount of energy needed to raise 1 kg of water from 15 degrees C to 16 degrees C

11. Which of the following BEST describes dietary thermogenesis?
    a. Energy needed for muscular work
    b. Energy use related to food ingestion
    c. Energy required to maintain normal body functions while at rest
    d. The amount of energy needed to raise 1 kg of water from 15 degrees C to 16 degrees C

12. Which of the following refers to energy that is needed for muscular work?
    a. Dietary thermogenesis
    b. The thermic effect of food
    c. Basal metabolism
    d. Physical activity calories

13. The amount of energy used by the body in digesting, absorbing, and transporting nutrients is called:
    a. dietary thermogenesis.
    b. adaptive thermogenesis.
    c. basal metabolic rate.
    d. calorie expenditure ratio.

14. The three major components of total energy expenditure in the body are:
    a. basal metabolism, adaptive thermogenesis, and resting activity.
    b. basal metabolism, physical activity, and sleep activity.
    c. basal metabolism, physical activity, and dietary thermogenesis.
    d. basal metabolism, adaptive thermogenesis, and physical activity.

15. Energy used to support body processes such as growth, health, tissue repair, and maintenance is called:
    a. adaptive thermogenesis.
    b. the thermic effect of food.
    c. basal metabolism.
    d. total energy expenditure.

16. The rate at which energy is used by the body when it is at complete rest is called:
    a. body composition.
    b. resting metabolic rate.
    c. sleeping metabolic rate.
    d. fasting metabolic rate.

17. Resting metabolic rate includes which of the following components?
    a. Energy for digestion
    b. Energy for physical activity
    c. Energy required for breathing
    d. Energy required to lift weights

18. Which of the following components of total energy expenditure accounts for 60 to 75% of total calorie needs in most people?
    a. Basal metabolism
    b. Physical activity
    c. Digestion of nutrients
    d. Absorption of nutrients

19. Dietary thermogenesis accounts for approximately what percentage of total energy expenditure?
    a. 60%
    b. 25%
    c. 10%
    d. 50%

20. Resting metabolic rate accounts for approximately what percentage of total energy use by the body?
    a. 60%
    b. 25%
    c. 10%
    d. 50%

21. Calories needed for basal metabolic processes in women can be estimated by:
    a. multiplying body weight in kilograms by 10.
    b. multiplying body weight in pounds by 10.
    c. multiplying body weight in kilograms by 11.
    d. multiplying body weight in pounds by 11.

22. Calories needed for basal metabolic processes in men can be estimated by:
    a. multiplying body weight in kilograms by 10.
    b. multiplying body weight in pounds by 10.
    c. multiplying body weight in kilograms by 11.
    d. multiplying body weight in pounds by 11.

23. Which of the following tissues and/or organs is the *least* metabolically active?
    a. Brain tissue
    b. Fat tissue
    c. Liver
    d. Muscle

44

24. Which of the components of total body energy expenditure can be influenced the most?
    a. Resting metabolic rate
    b. Energy of digestion
    c. Energy used in physical activity
    d. Energy used for sleep

25. Hunger can be defined as:
    a. unpleasant physical and psychological sensations that lead people to acquire and ingest food.
    b. a feeling of fullness or of having had enough to eat.
    c. the desire to eat aroused by thoughts of the taste and enjoyment of food.
    d. the desire to eat aroused by the sight or smell of food.

26. Satiety can be defined as:
    a. unpleasant physical and psychological sensations that lead people to acquire and ingest food.
    b. a feeling of fullness or of having had enough to eat.
    c. the desire to eat aroused by thoughts of the taste and enjoyment of food.
    d. the desire to eat aroused by the sight or smell of food.

27. Appetite can be defined as:
    a. unpleasant physical and psychological sensations that lead people to acquire and ingest food.
    b. a feeling of fullness or of having had enough to eat.
    c. the desire to eat aroused by thoughts of the taste and enjoyment of food.
    d. the desire to eat aroused by hunger pangs.

28. Weight loss occurs when:
    a. energy intake is greater than energy needs.
    b. energy intake is equal to energy needs.
    c. energy intake is less than energy needs.
    d. a person is in positive nitrogen balance.

29. A food containing 10 grams of fat, 6 grams of carbohydrate, and 24 grams of protein provides:
    a. 40 calories.
    b. 160 calories.
    c. 210 calories.
    d. 200 calories.

30. Which of the following nutrients contain 4 calories per gram?
    a. Alcohol and protein
    b. Water and carbohydrate
    c. Fat and carbohydrate
    d. Carbohydrate and protein

To check yourself, use the answer key at the bottom of the page.[9]

_____

[9] 1. c, 2. b, 3. a, 4. d, 5. b, 6. c, 7. a, 8. d, 9. d, 10. c, 11. b, 12. d, 13. a, 14. c, 15. c, 16. b, 17. c, 18. a, 19. c, 20. a, 21. b, 22. d, 23. b, 24. c, 25. a, 26. b, 27. c, 28. c, 29. c, 30. d

Unit 9 – Obesity to Underweight: The Highs and Lows of Weight Status

Key Concepts

- Ideal body weight and shape are defined by culture and by health measures. The operating definition should be based on health.
- Rates of overweight and obesity are increasing worldwide. Diseases and disorders related to excess body fat are also increasing.
- The location of body fat stores, as well as the amount of body fat, are important to health.
- The causes of obesity are complex and not completely understood. Diet, physical activity, environmental exposures, and genetic factors influence the development of obesity.
- Underweight in the United States usually results from a genetic tendency to be thin or from poverty, illness, or the voluntary restriction of food intake.

Unit Outline

I. Variations in body weight
II. How is weight status defined?
   A. Body mass index
      1. Assessing weight status in children and adolescents
   B. Most adults in the United States weigh too much
      1. The influence of obesity on health
      2. Obesity and psychological well-being
   C. Body fat and health: location, location, location
      1. Visceral fat and waist circumference
   D. Assessment of body fat content
      1. Methods for assessing body fat content
      2. Everybody needs some body fat
III. What causes obesity?
   A. Are some people born to be obese?
   B. Do obese children become obese adults?
   C. The role of diet in the development of obesity
      1. Low levels of physical activity promote obesity
IV. Obesity: the future lies in its prevention
   A. Preventing obesity in children
   B. Preventing obesity in adults
   C. Changing the environment
V. Some people are underweight
   A. Underweight defined
   B. Underweight and longevity in adults
VI. Toward a realistic view of body weight
   A. Size acceptance
      1. The Health at Every Size program

Unit Glossary

- **body mass index (BMI):** An indicator of the status of a person's weight for their height. It is calculated by dividing weight in kilograms by height in meters squared.
- **overweight:** A high weight-for-height.
- **obese:** A condition characterized by excess body fat.

46

- **metabolism:** The chemical changes that take place in the body. The conversion of glucose to energy or to body fat is an example of a metabolic process.
- **C-reactive protein (CRP):** A key inflammatory factor produced in the liver in response to infection or inflammation. Elevated concentrations of CRP are associated with heart disease, obesity, diabetes, inactivity, infection, smoking, and inadequate antioxidant intake.
- **subcutaneous fat** (Pronounced sub-q-tain-e-ous): Fat located under the skin.
- **visceral fat** (Pronounced vis-sir-el): Fat located under the skin and muscle of the abdomen.
- **chronic inflammation:** Low-grade inflammation that lasts weeks, months, or years. Inflammation is the first response of the body's immune system to infection or irritation. Inflammation triggers the release of biologically active substances that promote oxidation and other potentially harmful reactions in the body.
- **insulin resistance:** A condition in which cells "resist" the action of insulin in facilitating the passage of glucose into cells.
- **metabolic syndrome:** A constellation of metabolic abnormalities generally characterized by insulin resistance, abdominal obesity, high blood pressure and triglyceride levels, low levels of HDL cholesterol, and impaired glucose tolerance. Metabolic syndrome predisposes people to the development of type 2 diabetes, heart disease, hypertension, and other disorders. It is common—one in five U.S. adults has metabolic syndrome.
- **fatty liver disease:** A reversible condition characterized by fat infiltration of the liver (10% or more by weight). If not corrected, fatty liver disease can produce liver damage and other disorders. The condition is primarily associated with obesity, diabetes, and excess alcohol consumption. The disease is called "steatohepatitis" when accompanied by inflammation.
- **type 2 diabetes:** A disease characterized by high blood glucose levels due to the body's inability to use insulin normally or to produce enough insulin (previously called adult-onset diabetes).
- **environmental trigger:** An environmental factor, such as inactivity, a high-fat diet, or a high sodium intake, that causes a genetic tendency toward a disorder to be expressed.
- **underweight:** Usually defined as a low weight-for-height. May also represent a deficit of body fat.

Practice Multiple-Choice Test

1. Which of the following provides the best indicator of risk of death from all causes?
   a. Health insurance coverage
   b. Weight in pounds for age
   c. Weight for body frame size
   d. Body mass index

2. A person is underweight if their BMI is:
   a. 18.5-24.9 kg/m².
   b. 30 kg/m² or higher.
   c. under 18.5 kg/m².
   d. 25-29.9 kg/m².

3. Body mass index is calculated by:
   a. dividing weight in pounds by height in centimeters.
   b. dividing height in inches by weight in kilograms.
   c. dividing weight in kilograms by height in meters squared.
   d. dividing weight in kilograms by height in meters.

4. BMI percentile ranges for children and adolescents are used to assess:
   a. motor development.
   b. normal growth in terms of height.
   c. I.Q.
   d. weight status.

5. The combined incidence of overweight and obesity in the United States among adults is:
   a. 50%.
   b. 85%.
   c. 66%.
   d. 30%.

6. Among the following, the country with the highest prevalence rates of overweight and obesity is:
   a. China.
   b. France.
   c. Germany.
   d. Albania.

7. Fat located under the skin is specifically called:
   a. visceral fat.
   b. subcutaneous fat.
   c. baby fat.
   d. storage fat.

8. A pear body shape has all of the following characteristics EXCEPT:
   a. narrow shoulders.
   b. fat concentrated in the hips.
   c. high risk for heart disease compared to the apple shape.
   d. an average-sized waist.

9. An apple body shape has all of the following characteristics EXCEPT:
   a. fat concentrated in the waist.
   b. weight can be lost from the waist with diet and exercise.
   c. presence of visceral fat.
   d. low risk of heart disease.

10. A method of body fat assessment that uses an electrical current passing from the ankle to the wrist is called
    a. DEXA.
    b. MRI.
    c. BIA.
    d. skinfold measurement.

11. An indicator of the status of a person's weight for their height is called:
    a. basal metabolic rate.
    b. body mass index.
    c. body composition.
    d. body circumference index.

12. Type 2 diabetes, chronic inflammation, heart disease, and sleep disorders are all associated with:
    a. aging.
    b. physical activity.
    c. obesity.
    d. allergies.

13. Fat located under the skin and muscle of the abdomen is specifically called:
    a. visceral fat.
    b. subcutaneous fat.
    c. baby fat.
    d. storage fat.

14. A condition in which cells "resist" the action of insulin is called:
    a. type 1 diabetes.
    b. hypoglycemia.
    c. insulin resistance.
    d. ketosis.

15. A person with metabolic syndrome has all of the following characteristics EXCEPT:
    a. low body weight.
    b. insulin resistance.
    c. high blood pressure.
    d. low HDL levels.

16. A disease characterized by high blood glucose levels due to the body's inability to use insulin normally is called:
    a. juvenile diabetes.
    b. type 2 diabetes.
    c. high triglyceride syndrome.
    d. chronic inflammation.

17. An average body fat percentage for women is:
    a. less than 12%.
    b. less than 5%.
    c. greater than 35%.
    d. 32%.

18. An average body fat percentage for men is:
    a. 25% or more.
    b. less than 5%.
    c. 22%.
    d. 32%.

19. Skinfold thickness, underwater weighing, DEXA, and MRI are all methods used to determine:
    a. weight.
    b. bone density.
    c. chronological age.
    d. body fat content.

20. All of the following are methods for assessing body fat content EXCEPT:
    a. bioelectrical impedance.
    b. height-weight tables.
    c. dual-energy X-ray absorptiometry.
    d. whole body air displacement.

21. Science defines standards for body weight for adults based primarily on:
    a. cultural norms.
    b. societal influences.
    c. risk of death from all causes.
    d. weight-for-height tables.

22. An individual is considered overweight if their BMI is:
    a. 25-29.9 kg/m².
    b. under 18.5 kg/m².
    c. 18.5-24.9 kg/m².
    d. 30 kg/m² or higher.

23. An individual is considered of normal weight if their BMI is:
    a. 25-29.9 kg/m².
    b. under 18.5 kg/m².
    c. 18.5-24.9 kg/m².
    d. 30 kg/m² or higher.

24. Obesity in children and adolescents is assessed using:
    a. body fat content.
    b. BMI percentiles.
    c. weight-for-height tables.
    d. standard growth charts.

25. An obese person can decrease their health risks with a weight loss of approximately:
    a. 25% of body weight.
    b. 5 to 10% of body weight.
    c. 15% of body weight.
    d. Weight loss does not lower health risks.

26. All of the following are true regarding chronic inflammation EXCEPT:
    a. it is initiated by metabolic reactions in visceral fat.
    b. a person with an apple shape has a higher risk of developing it.
    c. it is more common in persons with a large percentage of subcutaneous fat.
    d. it increases the risk for insulin resistance and metabolic syndrome.

27. All of the following describe essential body fat EXCEPT:
    a. it serves a role in the manufacture of hormones.
    b. women need at least 10-12%
    c. it provides a cushion for organs.
    d. men need at least 10-12%.

50

28. A genetic trait predisposing one towards overweight is expressed after exposure to:
    a. the sight of fast food.
    b. marketing ploys.
    c. peer pressure.
    d. environmental triggers.

29. Causes of underweight include all of the following EXCEPT:
    a. insulin resistance.
    b. chronic disease.
    c. poverty.
    d. anorexia nervosa.

30. Prevention of obesity includes all of the following EXCEPT:
    a. making the environment more "friendly" to healthful choices.
    b. portion control.
    c. regular, vigorous exercise.
    d. lifelong calorie restriction.

To check yourself, use the answer key at the bottom of the page.[10]

---

[10] 1. d, 2. c, 3. c, 4. d, 5. c, 6. d, 7. b, 8. c, 9. d, 10. c, 11. b, 12. c, 13. a, 14. c, 15. a, 16. b, 17. d, 18. c, 19. d, 20. b, 21. c, 22. a, 23. c, 24. b, 25. c, 26. c, 27. d, 28. d, 29. a, 30. c

Unit 10 – Weight Control: The Myths and Realities

Key Concepts

- The effectiveness of weight-control methods should be gauged by their ability to prevent weight regain.
- That a weight-loss product or service is widely publicized and utilized doesn't mean it works.
- Successful weight control is characterized by gradual weight loss from small, acceptable, and individualized changes in eating and activity.

Unit Outline

I. Baseball, hot dogs, apple pie, and weight control
   A. Weight loss versus weight control
     1. The business of weight loss
     2. The lack of consumer protection
     3. Pulling the rug out
     4. What if the truth had to be told?
     5. Diet pills
II. Popular diets
   A. Fad diets
   B. Internet weight loss frauds
     1. Weight regain: a shared characteristic of popular diets
   C. Physical activity and weight control
   D. Weight loss benefits
   E. Obesity surgery
     1. Gastric bypass surgery
     2. Lap band surgery
       a. Concerns related to gastric bypass surgery
       b. Body contouring surgery
     3. Liposuction
III. Weight loss: making it last
   A. Small, acceptable changes
     1. Identifying small, acceptable changes
     2. What to expect for weight loss

Unit Glossary

- **bariatrics:** The field of medicine concerned with weight loss.

Practice Multiple-Choice Test

1. More than 29,000 weight-loss products are available for all of the following reasons EXCEPT:
   a. consumers want a quick fix.
   b. almost none of them work.
   c. there is a social pressure to be thin.
   d. they have all been tested for safety and are protected under federal law.

2. Features of weight-loss ads that make false or misleading claims include all of the following EXCEPT:
   a. promise of rapid weight loss.
   b. promise of an inexpensive product.
   c. use of testimonials.
   d. promise of long-term weight loss.

3. Which statement is true?
   a. Weight-loss products sold as supplements can be marketed without being tested for safety.
   b. You can trust an advertisement that promises safe, long-term weight loss.
   c. Weight-loss product manufacturers almost never violate truth-in-advertising laws.
   d. Xenical is a dietary supplement that was banned after it resulted in several deaths.

4. Most diets fail for all of the following reasons EXCEPT:
   a. they produce feelings of deprivation.
   b. they produce feelings of hunger.
   c. they can lead to depression.
   d. they are too easy to follow and get boring.

5. Approximately 90% of people who lose weight regain it because:
   a. they are no longer accepted by peers.
   b. the diet did not produce long-term changes in behavior.
   c. new clothes are too expensive.
   d. eating healthy is too expensive.

6. Weight that is lost through calorie reduction consists of:
   a. mostly water.
   b. 100% fat.
   c. water and fat.
   d. a combination of water, fat, and lean tissue.

7. One of the two most frequently performed weight-loss surgeries is:
   a. wiring of the jaw.
   b. liposuction.
   c. body contouring surgery.
   d. gastric bypass surgery.

8. All of the following are true regarding liposuction EXCEPT:
   a. it is considered cosmetic surgery and is not intended for weight loss.
   b. it reduces health risk factors such as high blood pressure.
   c. it is the most common type of cosmetic procedure in the U.S.
   d. surgical standards require that no more than 8 pounds of fat be removed.

9. Watching portion sizes and choosing lower-energy density foods are examples of:
   a. dramatic weight loss techniques.
   b. small, reasonable changes that will produce weight loss.
   c. weight control myths.
   d. the latest weight control fads.

10. A successful weight-loss program has all of the following characteristics EXCEPT:
    a. it is safe.
    b. it prevents weight regain.
    c. it focuses on lifestyle changes.
    d. it produces fast results.

11. An excess of 50 extra calories per day for one year will produce a weight gain of:
    a. No weight gain, it will even out
    b. 10 pounds.
    c. 5 pounds.
    d. 6 pounds.

12. Americans spend approximately how much on weight-loss products per year?
    a. $60 billion
    b. $60 million
    c. $60 trillion
    d. $600,000

13. On average, what percentage of U.S. adults are trying to lose weight on any given day?
    a. less than 10%
    b. 25%
    c. 75%
    d. 40%

14. Fraudulent weight-loss products may be investigated and taken off the market by which organization?
    a. USDA
    b. EPA
    c. FTC
    d. FDA

15. What is the main reason that amphetamines were removed from the weight-loss market?
    a. They did not work.
    b. They caused heart valve defects.
    c. They were highly addictive.
    d. They produced chronic diarrhea.

16. What is the main reason that Phen-Fen (Redux) was removed from the weight-loss market?
    a. It did not work.
    b. It caused heart valve defects.
    c. It was highly addictive.
    d. It produced chronic diarrhea.

17. Meridia (sibutramine) produces weight loss by:
    a. partially blocking fat absorption.
    b. melting fat.
    c. enhancing satiety.
    d. increasing metabolic rate.

18. Xenical (orlistat) produces weight loss by:
    a. partially blocking fat absorption.
    b. melting fat.
    c. enhancing satiety.
    d. increasing metabolic rate.

19. What two prescription drugs are approved for long-term use in obese people in the United States?
    a. Ephedra and sibutramine
    b. Hoodia and Meridian
    c. Orlistat and bitter orange
    d. Orlistat and sibutramine

20. Risks associated with use of prescription weight-loss medications include all of the following EXCEPT:
    a. oily stools.
    b. increased blood pressure.
    c. an increased desire to exercise.
    d. reduced absorption of fat-soluble vitamins.

21. All of the following are effects of weight loss EXCEPT:
    a. decreased levels of C-reactive protein.
    b. decreased levels of HDL.
    c. decreased blood insulin levels.
    d. decreased total cholesterol.

22. One of the biggest challenges in stemming the obesity epidemic is:
    a. preventing weight regain.
    b. weight loss.
    c. increasing availability of diet plans.
    d. decreasing fast food consumption.

23. The best indicator of successful weight-loss programs is:
    a. cost.
    b. location.
    c. long-term weight loss maintenance.
    d. number of lifestyle changes that need to be made.

24. Which statement about lap band surgery is false?
    a. Lap band surgery reduces stomach size by constricting the upper portion of the stomach.
    b. Lap band surgery patients tend to lose more weight than gastric bypass patients.
    c. Lap band surgery can be performed laparoscopically.
    d. The lap band apparatus is filled with saline solution, and can be drained or further inflated to adjust stomach size.

25. Bariatrics refers to:
    a. a type of chronic inflammation.
    b. a section of the intestinal tract.
    c. the field of medicine concerned with weight loss.
    d. the field of medicine concerned with colon health.

26. Weight-control surgery is reserved for:
    a. people with a BMI of 25-30.
    b. people with a BMI of 35 to 40 with no other health problems.
    c. people with a BMI of 20-25.
    d. people with a BMI > 40.

27. Gastric bypass surgery results in a stomach pouch that holds approximately:
    a. 2 tablespoons of food.
    b. 2 cups of food.
    c. 1 cup of food.
    d. ¾ cup of food.

28. All of the following are risks related to gastric bypass surgery EXCEPT:
    a. there is a 0.5-1.1% chance of dying.
    b. high blood pressure decreases.
    c. rates of complications are 40% within the first 6 months.
    d. vitamins and minerals are not absorbed properly.

29. After gastric bypass surgery, which vitamins and minerals are not absorbed properly?
    a. Magnesium and vitamin D
    b. Folate and sodium
    c. Vitamin B_{12} and iron
    d. Vitamin C and iron

30. All of the following are considered habits that lead to weight-loss maintenance EXCEPT:
    a. using popular diets.
    b. eating breakfast.
    c. choosing low-fat foods.
    d. keeping a food diary.

31. All of the following are considered habits that lead to regain of lost weight EXCEPT:
    a. exercising little.
    b. taking diet pills.
    c. making small changes in diet and physical activity.
    d. coping with stress by eating.

To check yourself, use the answer key at the bottom of the page.[11]

---

[11] 1. a, 2. b, 3. a, 4. d, 5. b, 6. d, 7. d, 8. b, 9. b, 10. d, 11. c, 12. a, 13. d, 14. c, 15. c, 16. b, 17. c, 18. a, 19. d, 20. c, 21. b, 22. a, 23. c, 24. b, 25. c, 26. d, 27. a, 28. b, 29. c, 30. a, 31. c

Unit 11 – Disordered Eating: Anorexia Nervosa, Bulimia, and Pica

Key Concepts

- Anorexia nervosa, bulimia nervosa (bulimia), binge-eating disorder, and pica are four specific eating disorders. They may seriously threaten health.
- Eating disorders are much more common in females than males.
- The incidence of eating disorders in a society is related to the value placed on thinness by that society.
- An important route to the prevention of anorexia nervosa and bulimia is to change a society's cultural ideal of thinness and to eliminate biases against people (especially women) who are not thin.

Unit Outline

I.   The eating disorders
   A. Anorexia nervosa
      1. The female athlete triad
      2. Motivations underlying anorexia nervosa
      3. What causes anorexia nervosa?
      4. How common is anorexia nervosa?
      5. Treatment
   B. Bulimia nervosa
      1. Is the cause of bulimia nervosa known?
      2. Treatment
   C. Binge-eating disorder
      1. The treatment approach to binge-eating disorder
   D. Resources for eating disorders
II. Undieting: the clash between culture and biology
III. Pica
   A. Geophagia
   B. Pagophagia
   C. Amylophagia
   D. Plumbism
   E. Proposed eating disorders

Unit Glossary

- **purging:** The use of self-induced vomiting, laxatives, or diuretics (water pills) to prevent weight gain.
- **anorexia nervosa:** An eating disorder characterized by extreme weight loss, poor body image, and irrational fears of weight gain and obesity.
- **binge eating:** The consumption of a large amount of food in a small amount of time.
- **bulimia nervosa:** An eating disorder characterized by recurrent episodes of rapid, uncontrolled eating of large amounts of food in a short period of time. Episodes of binge eating are often followed by purging.
- **restrained eating:** The purposeful restriction of food intake below desired amounts in order to control body weight.
- **binge-eating disorder:** An eating disorder characterized by periodic binge eating, which normally is not followed by vomiting or the use of laxatives. People must experience eating binges twice a week on average over a period of six months to qualify for the diagnosis.
- **pica** (pike-eh): The regular consumption of nonfood substances such as clay or laundry starch.

- **geophagia** (ge-oh-phag-ah): Clay or dirt eating.
- **pagophagia** (pa-go-phag-ah): Ice eating.
- **amylophagia** (am-e-low-phag-ah): Laundry starch or cornstarch eating.
- **plumbism:** Lead (primarily from old paint flakes) eating.

Practice Multiple-Choice Test

1. *Essential* features of anorexia nervosa include which of the following?
   a. Anemia and refusal to maintain body weight at or above 85% of normal weight
   b. Lack of menstrual cycle and intense fear of gaining weight
   c. Constipation and infertility
   d. Low bone density and thick facial hair

2. Females comprise approximately what percentage of all eating disorder cases?
   a. 100%
   b. 90%
   c. 80%
   d. 50%

3. A primary force underlying the development of eating disorders is thought to be:
   a. overabundance of cheap, unhealthy foods.
   b. pressure to conform to society's standard of beauty.
   c. desire for attention.
   d. avoidance of physical activity.

4. Groups of people at highest risk for developing anorexia nervosa include all of the following EXCEPT:
   a. discus throwers.
   b. ballet dancers.
   c. fitness instructors.
   d. people with type 1 diabetes.

5. The consumption of a large amount of food in a small amount of time is called:
   a. pigging out.
   b. binge-eating.
   c. being ravenous.
   d. closet eating.

6. All of the following are features of binge-eating disorder EXCEPT:
   a. 2 or more episodes of binge eating per week over a 6-month period.
   b. inability to stop eating.
   c. overall low caloric intake.
   d. post-binge feelings of self-hatred.

7. The regular consumption of nonfood substances such as clay or laundry starch is called:
   a. pica.
   b. galyphagia.
   c. amenorrhea.
   d. clayphagia.

58

8. Which of the following refers to the practice of eating lead, primarily from old paint flakes?
   a. Pagophagia
   b. Amylophagia
   c. Plumbism
   d. Geophagia

9. All of the following describe purging EXCEPT:
   a. self-induced vomiting.
   b. the use of laxatives to prevent weight gain.
   c. the consumption of nonfood substances.
   d. the use of diuretics to prevent weight gain.

10. All of the following are officially recognized as eating disorders EXCEPT:
    a. compulsive overeating.
    b. binge-eating disorder.
    c. anorexia nervosa.
    d. pica.

11. Symptoms of disordered eating include all of the following behaviors EXCEPT:
    a. feast and famine cycles.
    b. an occasional snack or missed meal.
    c. consumption of nonfood substances.
    d. binge-eating.

12. Features of anorexia nervosa include all of the following EXCEPT:
    a. extreme weight loss.
    b. poor body image.
    c. irrational fears of weight gain.
    d. elevated heart rate.

13. Males with anorexia nervosa typically have all of the following symptoms EXCEPT:
    a. low bone mass.
    b. substance abuse.
    c. decreased testosterone levels.
    d. increased sex drive.

14. Irregular or absent menstrual cycles in teenage females and women result in all of the following EXCEPT:
    a. osteoporosis later in life.
    b. delayed healing of bone and connective tissue injuries.
    c. increased risk of anemia.
    d. increased risk of bone fractures.

15. An eating disorder characterized by recurrent episodes of rapid, uncontrolled eating of a large amount of food followed by purging is called:
    a. restrained eating.
    b. binge-eating disorder.
    c. bulimia nervosa.
    d. anorexia nervosa.

16. *Essential* features of bulimia nervosa include all of the following EXCEPT:
    a. recurrent episodes of binge eating.
    b. recurrent use of purging to prevent weight gain.
    c. episodes occur at least 2 times a week for 3 months.
    d. tooth erosion.

17. The purposeful restriction of food intake below desired amounts in order to control body weight is defined as:
    a. "picky" eating.
    b. restrained eating.
    c. constrained eating.
    d. careful eating.

18. Tips to helping a person with an eating disorder include all of the following EXCEPT:
    a. gathering information about help services available.
    b. forcing the person to admit they have a problem.
    c. seeking emergency medical help in life-threatening situations.
    d. encouraging the person to express their feelings.

19. Which of the following refers to the practice of eating clay or dirt?
    a. Pagophagia
    b. Amylophagia
    c. Plumbism
    d. Geophagia

20. Which of the following refers to the practice of ice eating?
    a. Pagophagia
    b. Amylophagia
    c. Plumbism
    d. Geophagia

21. Which of the following refers to the practice of eating laundry starch or cornstarch?
    a. Pagophagia
    b. Amylophagia
    c. Plumbism
    d. Geophagia

22. Common features of pica include all of the following EXCEPT that it:
    a. occurs in young children in the southern United States.
    b. occurs in pregnant women in the southern United States.
    c. includes consumption of nonfood substances.
    d. includes cycles of purging.

23. Risks associated with the consumption of nonfood substances include all of the following EXCEPT:
    a. increased risk of lead poisoning.
    b. increased risk of ingestion of contaminants.
    c. increased risk of intestinal blockage.
    d. increased risk of sickle-cell anemia.

60

24. A cluster of symptoms which includes eating disorders, menstrual dysfunction, and decreased bone density in young female athletes is known as:
    a. bulimia athletica.
    b. the female athlete triad.
    c. the anorexia triad.
    d. anorexia athletica.

25. Causes of anorexia include all of the following EXCEPT:
    a. high self-esteem.
    b. a need for control.
    c. a desire for perfection.
    d. unhappiness.

26. Treatment for anorexia includes all of the following EXCEPT:
    a. psychological counseling.
    b. restoration of nutritional health.
    c. restoration of body shape.
    d. a short treatment program.

27. Bulimia nervosa occurs in approximately what percentage of young women?
    a. 5 to 8 %
    b. 1 to 3%
    c. 0.5%
    d. 7%

28. Anorexia nervosa occurs in approximately what percentage of young women?
    a. 1%
    b. 5%
    c. 0.5%
    d. 7%

29. Treatment for bulimia should include:
    a. psychological counseling only.
    b. a safe weight-loss program.
    c. nutrition and psychological counseling.
    d. nutrition counseling only.

30. Binge-eating disorder is more common in:
    a. underweight people.
    b. overweight and obese people.
    c. normal-weight people.
    d. underweight men.

To check yourself, use the answer key at the bottom of the page.[12]

---

[12] 1. b, 2. b, 3. b, 4. b, 5. b, 6. c, 7. a, 8. c, 9. c, 10. a, 11. b, 12. d, 13. d, 14. c, 15. c, 16. d, 17. b, 18. b, 19. d, 20. a, 21. b, 22. d, 23. d, 24. b, 25. a, 26. d, 27. b, 28. a, 29. c, 30. b

Unit 12 – Useful Facts about Sugars, Starches, and Fiber

Key Concepts

- Simple sugars, the "starchy" complex carbohydrates, and dietary fiber are members of the carbohydrate family.
- Ounce for ounce, sugars and the starchy complex carbohydrates supply fewer than half the calories of fat.
- Tooth decay and poor-quality diets are related to high sugar intake.
- Fiber benefits health in a number of ways.

Unit Outline

I. The carbohydrates
    A. Simple sugar facts
        1. Nutrition labeling of sugar?
        2. What's so bad about sugar?
        3. Advice on sugar intake
    B. The alcohol sugars—what are they?
    C. Artificial sweetener facts
        1. Saccharin
        2. Aspartame
            a. Is aspartame safe?
        3. Sucralose
        4. Acesulfame potassium
        5. Neotame
        6. Rebiana
    D. Complex carbohydrate facts
        1. Which foods have carbohydrates?
        2. Are they fattening?
        3. United States fiber facts
        4. Types of fiber
            a. Soluble and insoluble fiber
        5. Be cautious when adding more fiber to your diet
    E. Glycemic index of carbohydrates
    F. Carbohydrates and your teeth
        1. There's more to tooth decay than sugar per se
        2. Why does sugar promote tooth decay?
        3. Water fluoridation
        4. Baby bottle caries

Unit Glossary

- **carbohydrates:** Chemical substances in foods that consist of a simple sugar molecule or multiples of them in various forms.
- **simple sugars:** Carbohydrates that consist of a glucose, fructose, or galactose molecule, or a combination of glucose and either fructose or galactose. High-fructose corn syrup and alcohol sugars are also considered simple sugars. Simple sugars are often referred to as "sugars."
- **monosaccharides** (mono = one, saccharide = sugar): Simple sugars consisting of one sugar molecule. Glucose, fructose, and galactose are common examples of monosaccharides.

- **disaccharide** (di = two, saccharide = sugar): Simple sugars consisting of two molecules of monosaccharides linked together. Sucrose, maltose, and lactose are disaccharides.
- **glycogen:** The body's storage form of glucose. Glycogen is stored in the liver and muscles.
- **alcohol sugars:** Simple sugars containing an alcohol group in their molecular structure. The most common are xylitol, mannitol, and sorbitol. They are a subgroup of chemical substances called "polyols."
- **phenylketonuria** (feen-ol-key-toneu-re-ah), **PKU:** A rare genetic disorder related to the lack of the enzyme phenylalanine hydroxylase. Lack of this enzyme causes the essential amino acid phenylalanine to build up in blood.
- **complex carbohydrates:** The form of carbohydrate found in starchy vegetables, grains, and dried beans and in many types of dietary fiber. The most common form of starch is made of long chains of interconnected glucose units.
- **polysaccharides** (poly = many, saccharide = sugar): Carbohydrates containing many molecules of monosaccharides linked together. Starch, glycogen, and dietary fiber are the three major types of polysaccharides. Polysaccharides consisting of 3 to 10 monosaccharides may be referred to as oligosaccharides.
- **functional fiber:** Specific types of nondigestible carbohydrates that have beneficial effects on health. Two examples of functional fibers are psyllium and pectin.
- **dietary fiber:** Naturally occurring, intact forms of nondigestible carbohydrates in plants and "woody" plant cell walls. Oat and wheat bran, and raffinose in dried beans, are examples of this type of fiber.
- **total fiber:** The sum of functional and dietary fiber.
- **insulin resistance:** A condition is which cell membranes have a reduced sensitivity to insulin so that more insulin than normal is required to transport a given amount of glucose into cells.
- **type 2 diabetes:** A disease characterized by high blood glucose levels due to the body's inability to use insulin normally or to produce enough insulin.
- **glycemic index:** A measure of the extent to which blood glucose is raised by a 50-gram portion of a carbohydrate-containing food compared to 50 grams of glucose or white bread.
- **tooth decay:** The disintegration of teeth due to acids produced by bacteria in the mouth that feed on sugar. Also called dental caries or cavities.
- **plaque:** A soft, sticky, white material on teeth; formed by bacteria.

Practice Multiple-Choice Test

1. Carbohydrates consist of all of the following chemical substances EXCEPT:
   a. simple sugars.
   b. complex carbohydrates.
   c. fiber.
   d. alcohol.

2. The body's storage form of glucose is called:
   a. dextrose.
   b. blood sugar.
   c. glucagon.
   d. glycogen.

3. All of the following can be converted into glucose by the body EXCEPT:
   a. certain amino acids.
   b. fatty acids.
   c. monosaccharides.
   d. glycerol.

4. Sugars added to foods during processing are called:
   a. natural sugars.
   b. fortification.
   c. added sugars.
   d. enrichment.

5. All of the following are classified as simple sugars EXCEPT:
   a. monosaccharides.
   b. starches.
   c. disaccharides.
   d. glucose, fructose, and galactose.

6. All of the following are true regarding sugar alcohols EXCEPT:
   a. overconsumption can lead to intoxication.
   b. they are similar to simple sugars.
   c. they include xylitol, mannitol, and sorbitol.
   d. they provide 4 calories per gram.

7. All of the following are sugar substitutes used in the United States EXCEPT:
   a. sucralose.
   b. saccharin.
   c. cyclamate.
   d. rebiana.

8. The recommended daily intake of fiber for men and women 19-50 years old is:
   a. 28 and 35 grams per day, respectively.
   b. 19 and 25 grams per day, respectively.
   c. 12 and 19 grams per day, respectively.
   d. 12 and 13 grams per day, respectively.

9. The part of the grain that contains the most dietary fiber is the:
   a. germ.
   b. bran.
   c. endosperm.
   d. stalk.

10. Infants who routinely receive sweet fluids in bottles when they go to sleep develop:
    a. type 1 diabetes.
    b. glycemic overload.
    c. baby bottle caries.
    d. hyperactivity.

11. Carbohydrates provide:
    a. 2 calories per gram.
    b. 4 calories per gram.
    c. 6 calories per gram.
    d. 9 calories per gram.

64

12. For adults, the daily recommended level of carbohydrates is _____ of total calories:
    a. 15-25%
    b. 25-45%
    c. 35-55%
    d. 45-65%

13. Monosaccharides include all of the following EXCEPT:
    a. sucrose.
    b. glucose.
    c. fructose.
    d. galactose.

14. Disaccharides include all of the following EXCEPT:
    a. sucrose.
    b. lactose.
    c. galactose.
    d. maltose.

15. Which of the following are considered "chemical relatives" of carbohydrates?
    a. Ketones
    b. Alcohol and alcohol sugars
    c. Functional fibers
    d. High-fructose corn syrup

16. Another name for glucose is:
    a. sucrose.
    b. fructose.
    c. blood sugar.
    d. malitol.

17. The body primarily stores carbohydrates for later use in which two organs?
    a. Liver and muscles
    b. Kidney and muscles
    c. Gallbladder and liver
    d. Kidney and liver

18. The only simple sugar that the body can use directly to release energy is:
    a. fructose.
    b. sucrose.
    c. maltose.
    d. glucose.

19. A rare genetic disorder that causes phenylalanine to build up in the blood is called:
    a. sickle-cell anemia.
    b. phenylketonuria.
    c. fibromyalgia.
    d. ketosis.

20. All of the following describe complex carbohydrates EXCEPT:
    a. they include starches, glycogen, and dietary fiber.
    b. dietary sources include starchy vegetables, grains, and beans.
    c. animal products are considered a good source.
    d. they are also known as polysaccharides.

21. Carbohydrates containing many molecules of sugars linked together are called:
    a. monosaccharides.
    b. disaccharides.
    c. simple sugars.
    d. polysaccharides.

22. Specific types of nondigestible carbohydrates and connective tissues that have beneficial effects on health are called:
    a. dietary fiber.
    b. functional fiber.
    c. total fiber.
    d. sugar alcohols.

23. Naturally occurring, intact forms of nondigestible carbohydrates in plants and "woody" plant cell walls are called:
    a. dietary fiber.
    b. functional fiber.
    c. total fiber.
    d. sugar alcohols.

24. The sum of functional and dietary fiber is called:
    a. dietary fiber.
    b. functional fiber.
    c. total fiber.
    d. sugar alcohols.

25. All of the following are good sources of dietary fiber EXCEPT:
    a. avocado.
    b. fried chicken.
    c. oatmeal.
    d. almonds.

26. A condition in which cell membranes have a reduced sensitivity to insulin is called:
    a. glycemic state.
    b. caries.
    c. type 1 diabetes.
    d. insulin resistance.

27. A classification system that rates the extent to which carbohydrate-containing foods raise blood glucose is called the:
    a. functional fiber index.
    b. glycemic index.
    c. exchange system.
    d. monosaccharide index.

66

28. Diets providing low-glycemic index carbohydrates have been found to have all of the following benefits EXCEPT:
    a. reduction of elevated cholesterol.
    b. increased levels of HDL cholesterol.
    c. increased levels of triglycerides.
    d. decreased risk of developing type 2 diabetes.

29. Dental caries can be preventing by all of the following EXCEPT:
    a. brushing your teeth.
    b. drinking fluoridated water.
    c. increasing consumption of "sticky foods."
    d. using artificial sweeteners.

30. All of the following foods are considered to especially promote tooth decay EXCEPT:
    a. peanut butter.
    b. chewy cookies.
    c. pretzels.
    d. taffy.

To check yourself, use the answer key at the bottom of the page.[13]

_____

[13] 1. d, 2. d, 3. b, 4. c, 5. b, 6. a, 7. c, 8. a, 9. b, 10. c, 11. b, 12. d, 13. a, 14. c, 15. b, 16. c, 17. a, 18. d, 19. b, 20. c, 21. d, 22. b, 23. a, 24. c, 25. b, 26. d, 27. b, 28. c, 29. c, 30. a

Unit 13 – Diabetes Now

Key Concepts

- Diabetes is related to abnormal utilization of glucose by the body.
- The three main forms of diabetes are type 1, type 2, and gestational diabetes.
- Rates of type 2 diabetes increase as obesity does.
- Diet is always a part.
- Weight loss and physical activity can prevent or delay the onset of type 2 diabetes in many people.

Unit Outline

I. The diabetes epidemic
   A. Health consequences of diabetes
II. Type 2 diabetes
   A. Prediabetes
      1. Insulin resistance
      2. Metabolic syndrome
   B. Managing type 2 diabetes
      1. Glycemic index and glycemic load
         a. Glycemic load
   C. Sugar intake and diabetes
   D. Prevention of type 2 diabetes
III. Type 1 diabetes
   A. Managing type 1 diabetes
      1. Insulin and new technologies in the management of type 1 diabetes
IV. Gestational diabetes
V. Hypoglycemia: the low blood sugar blues?
VI. Diabetes in the future

Unit Glossary

- **diabetes:** A disease characterized by abnormal utilization of carbohydrates by the body and elevated blood glucose levels. There are three main types of diabetes: type 1, type 2, and gestational diabetes.
- **type 1 diabetes:** A disease characterized by high blood glucose levels resulting from destruction of the insulin-producing cells of the pancreas. This type of diabetes was called juvenile-onset diabetes and insulin-dependent diabetes in the past, and its official medical name is type 1 diabetes mellitus.
- **type 2 diabetes:** A disease characterized by high blood glucose levels due to the body's inability to use insulin normally, or to produce enough insulin. This type of diabetes was called adult-onset diabetes and noninsulin-dependent diabetes in the past, and its official medical name is type 2 diabetes mellitus.
- **gestational diabetes:** Diabetes first discovered during pregnancy.
- **chronic inflammation:** Low-grade inflammation that lasts weeks, months, or years. Inflammation is the first response of the body's immune system to infection or irritation. Inflammation triggers the release of biologically active substances that promote oxidation and other potentially harmful reactions in the body.
- **immune system:** Body tissues that provide protection against bacteria, viruses, foreign proteins, and other substances identified by cells as harmful.
- **insulin resistance:** A condition in which cell membranes have reduced sensitivity to insulin so that more insulin than normal is required to transport a given amount of glucose into cells. It is characterized by elevated levels of serum insulin, glucose, and triglycerides, and increased blood pressure.

- **prediabetes:** A condition in which blood glucose levels are higher than normal but not high enough for the diagnosis of diabetes. It is characterized by impaired glucose tolerance, or fasting blood glucose levels between 110 and 126 mg/dL.
- **fatty liver disease:** A reversible condition characterized by fat infiltration of the liver (10% or more by weight). If not corrected, fatty liver disease can produce liver damage and other disorders. The condition is primarily associated with obesity, diabetes, and excess alcohol consumption.
- **metabolic syndrome:** A constellation of metabolic abnormalities that increase the risk of heart disease and type 2 diabetes. Metabolic syndrome is characterized by insulin resistance, abdominal obesity, high blood pressure and triglycerides levels, low levels of HDL cholesterol, and impaired glucose tolerance. It is also called Syndrome X and insulin resistance syndrome.
- **glycemic index (GI):** A measure of the extent to which blood glucose level is raised by a 50-gram portion of a carbohydrate-containing food compared to 50 grams of glucose or white bread.
- **glycemic load (GL):** A measure of the extent to which blood glucose level is raised by a given amount of a carbohydrate-containing food. GL is calculated by multiplying a food's GI by its carbohydrate content.
- **glycemic load (GL):** A measure of the extent to which blood glucose level is raised by a given amount of a carbohydrate-containing food. GL is calculated by multiplying a food's GI by its carbohydrate content.
- **hypoglycemia:** A disorder resulting from abnormally low blood glucose levels. Symptoms of hypoglycemia include irritability, nervousness, weakness, sweating, and hunger.

Practice Multiple-Choice Test

1. A disease characterized by abnormal utilization of carbohydrates by the body and elevated blood glucose levels is called:
   a. hypoglycemia.
   b. plague.
   c. diabetes.
   d. chronic inflammation.

2. All of the following are among the recognized types of diabetes EXCEPT:
   a. gestational diabetes.
   b. hypertensive diabetes.
   c. type 1 diabetes.
   d. type 2 diabetes.

3. Risk factors for type 2 diabetes include all of the following EXCEPT:
   a. central obesity.
   b. inherited genetic traits.
   c. sedentary lifestyle.
   d. high simple sugar intake.

4. Type 2 diabetes is a result of all of the following EXCEPT:
   a. family history.
   b. obesity.
   c. physical inactivity.
   d. destruction of the insulin-producing pancreatic cells.

69

5. Prevention and management of metabolic syndrome should include all of the following EXCEPT:
   a. replacement of refined carbohydrates with complex carbohydrates.
   b. replacement of monounsaturated fats with saturated fats.
   c. physical activity.
   d. weight loss if obese.

6. Which of these foods has the lowest glycemic index?
   a. Honey
   b. Couscous
   c. Popcorn
   d. Pretzels

7. All of the following are steps that can be taken to decrease your risk for developing diabetes EXCEPT:
   a. choosing low-fat diary products.
   b. choosing low-glycemic index foods more often.
   c. consuming more whole grains than refined grains.
   d. consuming about 5 to 10 grams of fiber a day.

8. Treatment for type 1 diabetes typically includes all of the following EXCEPT:
   a. weight loss.
   b. insulin injections.
   c. regular meals and snacks.
   d. physical activity.

9. Type 1 diabetes accounts for approximately _____ of all cases
   a. 90-95%
   b. 80-90%
   c. 5-10%
   d. 10-20%

10. Diabetes that is first discovered during pregnancy is called:
    a. gestational.
    b. preeclampsia.
    c. type 1.
    d. hyperinsulinemia.

11. All of the following are adverse effects of high levels of blood glucose EXCEPT:
    a. chronic inflammation.
    b. elevated triglycerides.
    c. hardening of the arteries.
    d. increased HDL cholesterol.

12. Body tissues that provide protection against bacteria, viruses, and other harmful substances are called the:
    a. lymphatic system.
    b. immune system.
    c. circulatory system.
    d. nervous system.

70

13. Type 1 diabetes is _____.
    a. an obesity-related
    b. an acute disease
    c. an autoimmune disease
    d. a reversible condition

14. The first, direct result of destruction of pancreatic beta cells in an individual is:
    a. decreased levels of serum insulin.
    b. elevated levels of glucose.
    c. increased blood pressure.
    d. elevated levels of triglycerides.

15. Type 1 diabetes is characterized by high blood glucose levels resulting from:
    a. obesity.
    b. destruction of the insulin-producing cells of the pancreas.
    c. destruction of the insulin-producing cells of the liver.
    d. a sedentary lifestyle.

16. Approximately 90-95% of all cases of diabetes are:
    a. type 1.
    b. type 2.
    c. gestational.
    d. prediabetes.

17. Treatment for type 2 diabetes includes all of the following EXCEPT:
    a. weight loss of at least 15 to 20% of body weight.
    b. a diet high in complex carbohydrates.
    c. physical activity.
    d. regular snacks and meals.

18. A condition in which blood glucose levels are higher than normal but not high enough for the diagnosis of diabetes is called:
    a. metabolic syndrome.
    b. hypoglycemia.
    c. prediabetes.
    d. glycemic load.

19. The number one cause of death among people with diabetes is:
    a. kidney failure.
    b. old age.
    c. heart disease.
    d. stroke.

20. Diabetes is considered a(n):
    a. chronic disease.
    b. acute disease.
    c. infectious disease.
    d. contagious disease.

21. Metabolic syndrome is characterized by all of the following EXCEPT:
    a. elevated triglycerides.
    b. elevated HDL cholesterol.
    c. abdominal obesity.
    d. high blood pressure.

22. In order for a person to be first diagnosed with metabolic syndrome, _____ abnormalities must be present.
    a. one
    b. one to two
    c. three or more
    d. four or five

23. Adequacy of which 2 nutrients is considered especially important for prevention and management of metabolic system?
    a. Vitamin C and vitamin B_6
    b. Magnesium and iron
    c. Vitamin C and chromium
    d. Magnesium and vitamin D

24. Dietary management of diabetes should focus first on:
    a. blood glucose control.
    b. reduced sugar intake.
    c. increased physical activity.
    d. blood cholesterol control.

25. Glycemic index is a measure of:
    a. a protein-containing food's effect on blood glucose.
    b. a carbohydrate-containing food's effect on blood glucose.
    c. the amount of fiber a food contains.
    d. a food's carbohydrate calorie content.

26. Glycemic load is calculated by:
    a. multiplying a food's carbohydrate content by its protein content.
    b. multiplying a food's carbohydrate content by its fiber content.
    c. multiplying a food's GI by its protein content.
    d. multiplying a food's GI by its carbohydrate content.

27. A weight gain of _____ between the ages of 25 and 40 has been found to increase the risk of type 2 diabetes sevenfold.
    a. over 40 pounds
    b. 30 to 40 pounds
    c. 20 to 30 pounds
    d. 10 to 15 pounds

28. Type 1 diabetes has all of the following characteristics EXCEPT:
    a. it results form a deficiency of insulin.
    b. it usually occurs before age 40.
    c. it is associated with high levels of central body fat.
    d. it results due to a destruction of the beta cells in the pancreas.

72

29. A disorder resulting from abnormally low blood glucose levels is called:
   a. hyperglycemia.
   b. hypoglycemia.
   c. hypothyroidism.
   d. hyperpancreatitis.

30. Symptoms of hypoglycemia include all of the following EXCEPT:
   a. irritability.
   b. nervousness.
   c. weakness.
   d. elevated blood glucose.

To check yourself, use the answer key at the bottom of the page.[14]

---

[14] 1. c, 2. b, 3. d, 4. d, 5. b, 6. a, 7. d, 8. a, 9. c, 10. a, 11. d, 12. b, 13. c, 14. a, 15. b, 16. b, 17. a, 18. c, 19. c, 20. a, 21. b, 22. c, 23. d, 24. a, 25. b, 26. d, 27. d, 28. c, 29. b, 30. d

Unit 14 – Alcohol: The Positives and Negatives

Key Concepts

- Alcohol is both a food and a drug and can have positive or negative effects on health.
- Alcohol is produced from carbohydrates.
- Alcohol abuse is harmful to the body and is associated with a high proportion of acts of violence and accidents.
- Both genetic and environmental factors are associated with the development of alcoholism.

Unit Outline

I. Alcohol facts
    A. The positive
    B. The negative
    C. Alcohol intake, diet quality, and nutrient status
    D. How the body handles alcohol
        1. How to drink safely if you drink
    E. What causes alcoholism?
        1. Alcohol use among adolescents
        2. Help for alcohol dependence

Unit Glossary

- **fermentation:** The process by which carbohydrates are converted to ethanol by the action of the enzymes in yeast.
- **chronic inflammation:** Inflammation that is low-grade and lasts weeks, months, or years. Inflammation is the first response of the body's immune system to infection or irritation. It triggers the release of biologically active substances that promote oxidation and other potentially harmful reactions in the body.
- **alcoholism:** An illness characterized by a dependence on alcohol and by a level of alcohol intake that interferes with health, family and social relations, and job performance.
- **alcohol poisoning:** A condition characterized by mental confusion, vomiting, seizures, slow or irregular breathing, and low body temperature due to the effects of excess alcohol consumption. It is life-threatening and requires emergency medical help.
- **steatohepatitis** (pronounced ste-at-oh-hep-ah-tie-tis): A disease characterized by inflammation of, and fat accumulation in the liver. It is associated with alcoholism and may occur in obesity and diabetes. Steatohepatitis may progress to cirrhosis.
- **cirrhosis** (pronounced sear-row-sis): A disease of the liver characterized by widespread fibrous tissue buildup and disruption of normal liver structure and function. It can be caused by a number of chronic conditions that affect the liver.

Practice Multiple-Choice Test

1. All of the following are considered standard serving sizes of alcohol EXCEPT:
    a. 16 ounces of light beer.
    b. 12 ounces of regular beer.
    c. 5 ounces of wine.
    d. 1 ½ ounces of 80-proof alcohol.

74

2. A serving of alcohol contains:
   a. 0.5 ounces of alcohol.
   b. 0.6 ounces of alcohol.
   c. 0.7 ounces of alcohol.
   d. 0.8 ounces of alcohol.

3. Violence and injuries associated with alcohol include all of the following EXCEPT:
   a. homicide.
   b. drownings.
   c. road rage.
   d. traffic accidents.

4. Women who drink alcohol during pregnancy increase the risk of delivering a baby with:
   a. high birth weight.
   b. diabetes.
   c. high blood pressure.
   d. fetal alcohol syndrome.

5. Symptoms of fetal alcohol syndrome include all of the following EXCEPT:
   a. growth retardation.
   b. specific facial characteristics.
   c. mental retardation.
   d. wheat allergy.

6. Alcohol-containing beverages are considered to be:
   a. nutrient dense.
   b. empty calorie.
   c. high in complex carbohydrates.
   d. high in thiamin.

7. The legal limit for intoxication is:
   a. 0.03%.
   b. 0.04%.
   c. 0.05%.
   d. 0.08%.

8. Moderate consumption of alcohol for women is:
   a. 1 drink per day.
   b. 2 drinks per day.
   c. 3 drinks per day.
   d. 4 drinks per day.

9. The process by which carbohydrates are converted to ethanol is called:
   a. pasteurization.
   b. heat processing.
   c. fermentation.
   d. sterilization.

10. Alcohol is considered:
    a. a food but not a drug.
    b. a drug but not a food.
    c. a food and a drug.
    d. a good source of B vitamins.

11. All of the following are characteristics of alcoholism EXCEPT:
    a. dependence on alcohol.
    b. alcohol intake that interferes with family.
    c. alcohol intake that interferes with job performance.
    d. maintenance of good health.

12. All of the following describe symptoms of alcohol poisoning EXCEPT:
    a. slow or irregular breathing.
    b. high body temperature.
    c. mental confusion.
    d. seizures.

13. A life-threatening condition that is due to consumption of an excessive amount of alcohol in a short amount of time is known as:
    a. alcohol stupor.
    b. alcohol abuse.
    c. alcohol poisoning.
    d. alcohol overdose.

14. Habitually high levels of alcohol consumption increase the risk of developing all of the following EXCEPT:
    a. high blood pressure.
    b. thiamin toxicity.
    c. cirrhosis of the liver.
    d. cancer of the throat, stomach, and bladder.

15. A person who is an alcoholic will most likely be deficient in:
    a. protein, riboflavin, and zinc.
    b. vitamins C and E.
    c. calcium and magnesium.
    d. thiamin, vitamin A, and folate.

16. Alcohol provides:
    a. 7 calories per gram.
    b. 5 calories per gram.
    c. 4 calories per gram.
    d. no calories.

17. All of the following are steps that should be taken if you suspect someone has alcohol poisoning EXCEPT:
    a. make them drink strong coffee.
    b. call 911.
    c. seek help before all the symptoms appear.
    d. do not assume the person can "sleep it off."

18. Which of the following is the best recommendation concerning alcohol intake for women who are or may become pregnant?
    a. Limit drinks to 1 per day
    b. Only drink light beer or wine coolers
    c. Drink only during the last trimester
    d. Do not drink

19. Delirium tremens, known as the "DTs," is a result of:
    a. thiamin toxicity.
    b. niacin toxicity.
    c. thiamin deficiency.
    d. niacin deficiency.

20. Symptoms of delirium tremens include all of the following EXCEPT:
    a. convulsions.
    b. hallucinations.
    c. confusion.
    d. high HDL cholesterol levels.

21. Drinking responsibly includes all of the following recommendations EXCEPT:
    a. limiting alcohol to one drink per day if pregnant.
    b. slowly sipping rather than gulping drinks.
    c. not drinking on an empty stomach.
    d. never driving under the influence of alcohol.

22. The term *proof* originated from the practice of:
    a. testing whether an alcohol-containing liquid would ignite.
    b. testing whether an alcohol-containing liquid tasted good.
    c. testing the color of an alcohol-containing liquid.
    d. testing how much of an alcohol-containing liquid would lead to intoxication.

23. The type of alcohol consumed is:
    a. isopropanol.
    b. xylitol.
    c. methanol.
    d. ethanol.

24. Benefits of alcohol include which of the following?
    a. Improved mood
    b. Increased HDL levels
    c. Increased complex carbohydrate intake
    d. Decreased anxiety

25. Moderate consumption of alcohol for men is:
    a. 1 drink per day.
    b. 2 drinks per day.
    c. 3 drinks per day.
    d. 4 drinks per day.

26. Red wine is thought to reduce the risk of heart disease for all of the following reasons EXCEPT:
    a. the pigments act as antioxidants.
    b. it improves circulatory function.
    c. it helps prevent the formation of plaque in the arteries.
    d. it lowers blood pressure.

27. Heavy drinking is defined as:
    a. 2 drinks per day.
    b. 3 drinks per day.
    c. 4 drinks per day.
    d. 5 or more drinks per day.

28. Risk of heart disease can be reduced without alcohol by all of the following EXCEPT:
    a. drinking purple grape juice.
    b. following a diet low in *trans* fats.
    c. avoiding physical activity.
    d. not smoking.

29. Alcohol is absorbed rapidly in the:
    a. stomach and small intestine.
    b. large intestine.
    c. liver.
    d. kidneys.

30. Which of the following statements regarding alcoholism is true?
    a. One in three adults in the U.S. abuses alcohol.
    b. A person who begins to drink alcohol at age 15 is at much higher risk for developing alcohol dependency than a person who waits until age 21.
    c. While the rate of alcohol use among adolescents is increasing, the average age at which drinking begins is going up.
    d. Alcoholism is caused entirely by environmental influences.

To check yourself, use the answer key at the bottom of the page.[15]

---

[15] 1. a, 2. b, 3. c, 4. d, 5. d, 6. b, 7. d, 8. a, 9. c, 10. c, 11. d, 12. b, 13. c, 14. b, 15. d, 16. a, 17. a, 18. d, 19. c, 20. d, 21. a, 22. a, 23. d, 24. b, 25. b, 26. d, 27. d, 28. c, 29. a, 30. b

Unit 15 – Proteins and Amino Acids

Key Concepts

- Proteins are made of amino acids. Some amino acids are "essential" (required in the diet), and some are "nonessential" (not a required part of diets).
- Although protein can be used for energy, its major functions in the body involve the construction, maintenance, and repair of protein tissues.
- Protein tissue construction in the body proceeds only when all nine essential amino acids are available.
- Appropriate combinations of plant foods can supply sufficient quantities of all the essential amino acids.

Unit Outline

I. Protein's image versus reality
   A. Functions of protein
II. Amino acids
   A. Proteins differ in quality
      1. Complete proteins
      2. Vegetarian diets
   B. Amino acid supplements
      1. Amino acid supplements and muscle mass
III. Food as a source of protein
   A. What happens when a diet contains too little protein?
   B. How much protein is too much?

Unit Glossary

- **protein:** Chemical substance in foods made up of chains of amino acids.
- **hormone:** A substance, usually a protein or steroid (a cholesterol-derived chemical), produced by one tissue and conveyed by the bloodstream to another. Hormones affect the body's metabolic processes such as glucose utilization and fat deposition.
- **immunoproteins:** Blood proteins such as phagocytes (pronounced fag-o-sites) and antibodies that play a role in the functioning of the immune system (the body's disease defense system). White blood cells are a type of phagocyte that engulfs and absorbs foreign bodies and harmful organisms in blood and tissues. Antibodies attack foreign proteins.
- **DNA** (deoxyribonucleic acid): Genetic material contained in cells that initiates and directs the production of proteins in the body.
- **essential amino acids:** Amino acids that cannot be synthesized in adequate amounts by humans and therefore must be obtained from the diet. They are sometimes referred to as "indispensable amino acids."
- **nonessential amino acids:** Amino acids that can be readily produced by humans from components of the diet. Also referred to as "dispensable amino acids."
- **complete proteins:** Proteins that contain all of the essential amino acids in amounts needed to support growth and tissue maintenance.
- **incomplete proteins:** Proteins that are deficient in one or more essential amino acids.
- **kwashiorkor:** A form of severe protein-energy malnutrition in young children. It is characterized by swelling, fatty liver, susceptibility to infection, profound apathy, and poor appetite. The cause of kwashiorkor is unclear.

79

Practice Multiple-Choice Test

1. All of the following are true regarding the functions that proteins serve in the body EXCEPT:
   a. they serve as structural components.
   b. they serve as enzymes.
   c. they serve as hormones.
   d. they serve as the sole source of energy.

2. Diets high in protein are generally accompanied by:
   a. high fat and low fiber intakes.
   b. high fat and high fiber intakes.
   c. low fat and low fiber intakes.
   d. low fat and high fiber intakes.

3. A chemical substance in foods made up of chains of amino acids is called:
   a. triglycerides.
   b. protein.
   c. monosaccharides.
   d. hormones.

4. Which of the following foods is a good source of complete protein?
   a. Rice
   b. Corn
   c. Cottage cheese
   d. Tortillas

5. Sources of incomplete proteins include all of the following EXCEPT:
   a. rice.
   b. milk.
   c. beans.
   d. corn.

6. Amino acid supplements should be used with caution for all of the following reasons EXCEPT:
   a. their purity is not guaranteed.
   b. the dose provided by each pill is not guaranteed.
   c. the evidence from long-term safety studies.
   d. their effectiveness is not guaranteed.

7. Which of the following amino acid supplements is currently banned in the U.S.?
   a. Methionine
   b. Tryptophan
   c. Tyrosine
   d. Melatonin

8. The best way to build muscle is to:
   a. eat a very-high-protein diet.
   b. take amino acid supplements.
   c. exercise and eat a balanced diet.
   d. avoid high-protein foods after exercise.

80

9. A form of protein-energy malnutrition characterized by swelling and fatty liver is called:
   a. rabbit fever.
   b. marasmus.
   c. kwashiorkor.
   d. bulimia.

10. A complex illness that results from excessive protein intake is called:
    a. rabbit fever.
    b. marasmus.
    c. kwashiorkor.
    d. bulimia.

11. Proteins contain:
    a. 7 calories per gram.
    b. 9 calories per gram.
    c. 5 calories per gram.
    d. 4 calories per gram.

12. Blood proteins that play a role in the body's defense against infectious disease are called:
    a. enzymes.
    b. hormones.
    c. immunoproteins.
    d. hemoglobin.

13. Amino acids that cannot be made in adequate amounts by the body and must be consumed in the diet are called:
    a. nonessential amino acids.
    b. dispensable amino acids.
    c. essential amino acids.
    d. necessary amino acids.

14. There are _____ common amino acids.
    a. 19
    b. 20
    c. 9
    d. 11

15. Amino acids that can be readily produced in humans from the components of the diet are called:
    a. indispensable amino acids.
    b. essential amino acids.
    c. unimportant amino acids.
    d. nonessential amino acids.

16. Of the common amino acids, _____ are considered essential.
    a. 11
    b. 10
    c. 9
    d. 8

17. Which of the following is true regarding essential amino acids?
    a. They must be consumed in the diet.
    b. You can only get them by taking supplements.
    c. The body can make them.
    d. They are not required in the diet.

18. Genetic material contained in cells that initiates and directs the production of proteins in the body is called:
    a. hormones.
    b. enzymes.
    c. phagocytes.
    d. deoxyribonucleic acid.

19. Of the common amino acids, _____ are considered nonessential.
    a. 11
    b. 10
    c. 9
    d. 8

20. Proteins that are deficient in one or more essential amino acids are called:
    a. high-quality proteins.
    b. complete proteins.
    c. incomplete proteins.
    d. animal proteins.

21. Proteins that contain all of the essential amino acids in amounts needed to support growth and tissue maintenance are called:
    a. complete proteins.
    b. plant proteins.
    c. important proteins.
    d. low-quality proteins.

22. Sources of complete proteins for adults include all of the following EXCEPT:
    a. soybeans.
    b. fish.
    c. eggs.
    d. black beans.

23. High-protein diets have been implicated in the development of all of the following EXCEPT:
    a. kidney stones.
    b. heart disease.
    c. cancer.
    d. underweight.

24. The RDA for protein for men aged 19 to 24 years is:
    a. 46 grams.
    b. 56 grams.
    c. 75 grams.
    d. 82 grams.

25. The RDA for protein for women aged 19 to 24 years is:
    a. 46 grams.
    b. 56 grams.
    c. 75 grams.
    d. 82 grams.

26. On average, Americans obtain approximately _____ of total calories from protein.
    a. 45%
    b. 35%
    c. 25%
    d. 15%

27. Proteins differ from carbohydrates and fats due to the fact that:
    a. proteins are found in milk.
    b. proteins contain nitrogen.
    c. proteins cannot be used for energy.
    d. proteins are found in beans and grains.

28. How well dietary proteins support tissue construction is called:
    a. protein quantity.
    b. protein quality.
    c. protein worth.
    d. protein superiority.

29. A standard serving size of a high-protein food is approximately:
    a. 3 ounces.
    b. 4 ounces.
    c. 6 ounces.
    d. 7 ounces.

30. Protein foods are also generally high in all of the following EXCEPT:
    a. iron.
    b. zinc.
    c. vitamin B_{12}.
    d. fiber.

To check yourself, use the answer key at the bottom of the page.[16]

---

[16] 1. d, 2. b, 3. b, 4. c, 5. b, 6. c, 7. b, 8. c, 9. c, 10. a, 11. d, 12. c, 13. c, 14. b, 15. d, 16. c, 17. a, 18. d, 19. a, 20. c, 21. a, 22. d, 23. d, 24. b, 25. a, 26. d, 27. b, 28. b, 29. a, 30. d

Unit 16 – Vegetarian Diets

Key Concepts

- Vegetarianism is more than a diet. It is often part of a value system that influences a variety of attitudes and behaviors.
- Appropriately planned vegetarian diets are health promoting.
- Vegetarian diets that lead to caloric and nutrient deficiencies generally include too narrow a range of foods.

Unit Outline

I. Perspectives on vegetarianism
    A. Reasons for vegetarianism
        1. Vegetarian diets come in many types
        2. Vegetarian diet options
            a. Macrobiotic diets
            b. Raw food diets
            c. Other vegetarian diets
    B. Vegetarian diets and health
    C. What are the health benefits of vegetarian diets?
II. Dietary recommendations for vegetarians
    A. Well-planned vegetarian diets
        1. Complementary protein foods
    B. Where to go for more information on vegetarian diets

Unit Glossary

- **fruitarian:** A form of vegetarian diet in which fruits are the major ingredient. Such diets provide inadequate amounts of a variety of nutrients.
- **complete proteins:** Proteins that contain all of the nine essential amino acids in amounts sufficient to support protein tissue construction by the body.
- **essential amino acids:** Amino acids that cannot be synthesized in adequate amounts by the human body and must therefore be obtained from the diet.
- **complementary protein sources:** Plant sources of protein that together provide sufficient quantities of the nine essential amino acids.

Practice Multiple-Choice Test

1. Most of the world's population subsists on vegetarian diets because:
    a. meat and other animal products are scarce or too expensive.
    b. cattle are too difficult to farm.
    c. animals are free range and hard to capture.
    d. hormones and antibiotics are not available to treat the meats.

2. All of the following are reasons that people choose to follow a vegetarian diet EXCEPT:
    a. health.
    b. religious beliefs.
    c. desire to "eat high on the food chain."
    d. desire to preserve the world's food supply.

84

3. All of the following are good vegetarian sources of vitamin B$_{12}$, calcium, vitamin D, and EPA/DHA EXCEPT:
   a. soy milk and rice milk.
   b. fortified breakfast cereals.
   c. supplements.
   d. romaine lettuce.

4. The least restrictive form of "vegetarian" diet excludes only red meat and is called:
   a. vegan.
   b. far vegetarian.
   c. macrobiotic.
   d. quasi-vegetarian.

5. Which two types of vegetarian diets include only plant foods?
   a. Far vegetarian and raw food dieters
   b. Quasi-vegetarians and vegans
   c. Vegans and raw food dieters
   d. Lacto-vegetarians and lacto-ovo vegetarians

6. Important recommendations for vegetarians include all of the following EXCEPT:
   a. ensure an adequate amount of calories.
   b. eat a varied diet.
   c. eat a balanced diet.
   d. eat only nonfat foods.

7. All of the following are nutrients that are likely to be lacking in the diets of vegetarians EXCEPT:
   a. vitamin D.
   b. calcium.
   c. vitamin C.
   d. EPA and DHA.

8. All of the following are examples of complementary proteins EXCEPT:
   a. corn and dried beans.
   b. rice and green peas.
   c. bananas and apples.
   d. soybeans and seeds.

9. Reasons that people follow vegetarian diets include which of the following?
   a. To lower disease risk and maintain weight
   b. To lower disease risk and gain weight
   c. To lower cholesterol and increase intake of antibiotics
   d. To lower disease risk and eat high on the food chain

10. People who are vegetarians tend to also engage in which of the following?
    a. Tobacco use
    b. Alcohol use
    c. Illicit drug use
    d. Physical activity

11. Quasi-vegetarian diets exclude which of the following?
    a. Poultry
    b. Fish
    c. Dairy
    d. Eggs

12. Lacto-ovo vegetarian diets include all of the following EXCEPT:
    a. dairy products.
    b. eggs.
    c. plant foods.
    d. fish.

13. Lacto-vegetarian diets include all of the following EXCEPT:
    a. milk.
    b. milk products.
    c. pork.
    d. plant foods.

14. Vegans may avoid all of the following EXCEPT:
    a. eating plant foods.
    b. eating honey.
    c. wearing clothes made from leather.
    d. drinking cow's milk.

15. All of the following are true regarding macrobiotic diets EXCEPT:
    a. some forms are only quasi-vegetarian.
    b. "yin" and "yang" foods are balanced.
    c. locally grown whole foods are emphasized.
    d. specific foods are prohibited.

16. Raw food diets are based on the misconception that:
    a. cooking destroys all of the nutrients in foods.
    b. cooking "hurts" plants.
    c. enzymes in raw food promote normal digestion.
    d. cooking takes too much time.

17. Raw food diets have been shown to have all of the following detrimental effects EXCEPT:
    a. impaired growth.
    b. lower HDL cholesterol levels.
    c. lower bone mineral density.
    d. higher triglyceride levels.

18. A form of vegetarian diet in which fruits are the major ingredient is called:
    a. appletarian.
    b. fruitarian.
    c. the raw food diet.
    d. foodie.

19. Proteins that contain all of the essential amino acids in amounts sufficient to support tissue construction in the body are called:
    a. very important proteins.
    b. incomplete proteins.
    c. inadequate proteins.
    d. complete proteins.

20. EPA and DHA are two important fatty acids found primarily in:
    a. fish and seafood.
    b. dairy and meat.
    c. cheese and plants.
    d. eggs and beans.

21. All of the following are health benefits of following a vegetarian diet EXCEPT:
    a. lower risk of heart disease.
    b. lower risk of stroke.
    c. lower risk of type 2 diabetes.
    d. lower fiber intake.

22. Amino acids that cannot be synthesized in adequate amounts by the human body and must be obtained in the diet are called:
    a. nonessential amino acids.
    b. unnecessary amino acids.
    c. essential amino acids.
    d. critical amino acids.

23. Plant sources of protein that together provide sufficient quantities of the essential amino acids are called:
    a. paired proteins.
    b. complementary proteins.
    c. harmonizing proteins.
    d. matching proteins.

24. Examples of meals that contain complete proteins include all of the following EXCEPT:
    a. carrots and mushrooms.
    b. tofu and rice.
    c. tortilla and refried beans.
    d. bulgur and lentils.

25. Bean cuisine is important in many cultures and examples include all of the following EXCEPT:
    a. hummus.
    b. chili.
    c. bulgur.
    d. baked beans.

26. Complete proteins are found in all of the following EXCEPT:
    a. meat.
    b. eggs.
    c. zucchini.
    d. milk.

27. The only plant protein that contains all nine essential amino acids is:
    a. green beans.
    b. romaine lettuce.
    c. soybeans.
    d. lima beans.

28. All of the following are true regarding essential amino acids EXCEPT:
    a. they are needed to replace red blood cells.
    b. the body can store them for several months.
    c. they are needed in the diet.
    d. they are needed to repair tissues.

29. Typically, vegetarians' absorption of iron from plant foods is enhanced by their ample:
    a. vitamin D intake.
    b. vitamin C intake.
    c. B vitamin intake.
    d. vitamin A intake.

30. Which nutrient has consistently been shown to be lacking in the diets of individuals who do not consume animal products?
    a. Thiamin
    b. Fiber
    c. Vitamin B_{12}
    d. Vitamin C

To check yourself, use the answer key at the bottom of the page.[17]

_____

[17] 1. a, 2. c, 3. d, 4. b, 5. c, 6. d, 7. c, 8. c, 9. a, 10. d, 11. a, 12. d, 13. c, 14. a, 15. d, 16. c, 17. d, 18. b, 19. d, 20. a, 21. d, 22. c, 23. b, 24. a, 25. c, 26. c, 27. c, 28. b, 29. b, 30. c

Unit 17 – Food Allergies and Intolerances

Key Concepts

- True food allergies involve a response by the body's immune system to a particular substance in food.
- Food allergies may be caused by hundreds of different foods. However, 90% of food allergies are due to eight foods: nuts, eggs, wheat, milk, peanuts, soy, shellfish, and fish.
- Food intolerances cover an array of adverse reactions that do *not* involve the body's immune system.
- The most accurate method of identifying food allergies and intolerances in most cases is the double-blind, placebo-controlled food challenge.

Unit Outline

I. Food allergy mania
   A. Adverse reactions to foods
      1. Why do food allergies involve the immune system?
      2. What foods are most likely to cause allergic reactions?
         a. A closer look at wheat allergy
   B. How common are food allergies?
II. Diagnosis: Is it a food allergy?
   A. The other tests for food allergy
      1. Immunoglobulin E tests
      2. Skin prick tests
      3. Bogus tests
   B. What's the best way to treat food allergies?
III. Food intolerances
   A. Lactose maldigestion and intolerance
   B. Sulfite sensitivity
   C. Red wine, aged, cheese, and migraines
   D. MSG and the "Chinese restaurant syndrome"
IV. Precautions

Unit Glossary

- **food allergy:** Adverse reaction to a normally harmless substance in food that involves the body's immune system. (Also called food hypersensitivity.)
- **immune system:** Body tissues that provide protection against bacteria, viruses, and other substances identified by cells as harmful.
- **food intolerance:** Adverse reaction to a normally harmless substance in food that does not involve the body's immune system.
- **food allergen:** A substance in food (almost always a protein) that is identified as harmful by the body and elicits an allergic reaction from the immune system.
- **antibodies:** In the case of allergies, proteins the body makes to combat allergens.
- **histamine** (hiss-tah-mean): A substance released in allergic reactions. It causes dilation of blood vessels, itching, hives, and a drop in blood pressure and stimulates the release of stomach acids and other fluids. Antihistamines neutralize the effects of histamine and are used in the treatment of some cases of allergies.
- **anaphylactic shock** (an-ah-fa-lac-tic): Reduced oxygen supply to the heart and other tissues due to the body's reaction to an allergen in food or other "foreign" substance. Symptoms of anaphylactic

shock (or "anaphylaxis") may include abdominal cramps, vomiting, chest tightness, paleness, weak and rapid pulse, and difficulty breathing.

- **celiac disease:** An autoimmune disease characterized by inflammation of the small intestine lining resulting from a genetically based intolerance to gluten. The inflammation produces diarrhea, fatty stools, weight loss, and vitamin and mineral deficiencies. (Also called celiac sprue and gluten-sensitive enteropathy.)
- **autoimmune disease:** A disease related to the destruction of the body's own cells by substances produced by the immune system that mistakenly recognize certain cell components as harmful.
- **double-blind, placebo-controlled food challenge:** A test used to determine the presence of a food allergy or other adverse reaction to a food. In this test, neither the patient nor the care provider knows whether a suspected offending food or a placebo is being tested.
- **lactose maldigestion:** A disorder characterized by reduced digestion of lactose due to the low availability of the enzyme lactase.
- **lactose intolerance:** The term for gastrointestinal symptoms (flatulence, bloating, abdominal pain, diarrhea, and "rumbling in the bowel") resulting from the consumption of more lactose than can be digested with available lactase.

Practice Multiple-Choice Test

1. A substance in food that is identified as harmful by the body and elicits an allergic reaction from the immune system is called a:
   a. food toxin.
   b. food poisoning.
   c. food allergen.
   d. food pollutant.

2. The development of allergic reactions involves all of the following EXCEPT:
   a. consumption of a food allergen by susceptible people.
   b. antibody formation.
   c. histamine release.
   d. antioxidant release.

3. All of the following are common symptoms caused by food allergies EXCEPT:
   a. rash or hives.
   b. gastrointestinal upsets.
   c. respiratory problems.
   d. central nervous system problems.

4. All of the following foods are known to cause anaphylactic shock in highly sensitive people EXCEPT:
   a. eggs.
   b. cabbage.
   c. nuts.
   d. fish.

5. Proteins the body makes to combat allergens are called:
   a. hormones.
   b. red blood cells.
   c. antibodies.
   d. antioxidants.

90

6. Approximately 90% of all food allergies are caused by which eight foods?
   a. Nuts, eggs, honey, wheat, milk, peanuts, fish, shellfish
   b. Nuts, peanuts, eggs, wheat, bulgur, milk, fish, shellfish
   c. Nuts, peanuts, eggs, wheat, milk, soy, shellfish, fish
   d. Nuts, eggs, honey, soy, wheat, milk, fish, shellfish

7. Non-"gold standard" tests for food allergies that vary in reliability from slightly accurate to bogus include all of the following EXCEPT:
   a. double-blind placebo controlled food challenge.
   b. skin prick tests.
   c. hair analysis.
   d. immunoglobulin E tests.

8. All of the following are true regarding sulfites EXCEPT:
   a. small amounts can cause anaphylactic shock in sensitive people.
   b. the FDA requires that sulfites must be listed on food labels.
   c. the FDA allows sulfites to only be used on fresh fruits and vegetables.
   d. sources of sulfites include red wine, dried fruit, canned vegetables.

9. An adverse reaction to a normally harmless substance in food that involves the body's immune system is called a:
   a. food intolerance.
   b. food reaction.
   c. food allergy.
   d. food tolerance.

10. Which term refers to body tissues that provide protection against bacteria, viruses, and other harmful substances?
    a. Antioxidants
    b. Free radicals
    c. Immune system
    d. Lymphatic system

11. An adverse reaction to a normally harmless substance in food that does *not* involve the body's immune system is a:
    a. food intolerance.
    b. food reaction.
    c. food allergy.
    d. food tolerance.

12. Another term used to describe a food allergy is:
    a. food concern.
    b. food hypersensitivity.
    c. food intolerance.
    d. food reaction.

13. A substance released in allergic reactions that causes itching and hives is called:
    a. antihistamine.
    b. histamine.
    c. a beta blocker.
    d. an allergen.

14. All of the following describe actions that histamine produces EXCEPT:
    a. a rise in blood pressure.
    b. a drop in blood pressure.
    c. hives and itching.
    d. dilation of blood vessels.

15. A reduction in blood supply to the heart and other tissues due to the body's reaction to a substance in food is called:
    a. lactose intolerance.
    b. food intolerance.
    c. histamine shock.
    d. anaphylactic shock.

16. All of the following are symptoms of anaphylactic shock EXCEPT:
    a. strong and slow pulse.
    b. paleness.
    c. chest tightness.
    d. difficulty breathing.

17. A disease characterized by inflammation of the small intestine lining resulting from a genetically based intolerance to gluten is called:
    a. gluten allergy.
    b. celiac disease.
    c. Crohn's disease.
    d. irritable bowl syndrome.

18. The "gold standard" for diagnosing food allergies is called the:
    a. immunoglobulin E test.
    b. experimental food challenge.
    c. skin prick test.
    d. double-blind placebo-controlled food challenge.

19. In the double-blind placebo-controlled food challenge:
    a. only the care provider knows whether a suspected food is being tested.
    b. the patient and the care provider know whether a suspected food is being tested.
    c. the patient knows whether a suspected food or placebo is being tested.
    d. neither the patient nor the care provider knows whether a suspected food or placebo is being tested.

20. A disorder characterized by reduced digestion of lactose due to the low availability of the enzyme lactase is called:
    a. lactose intolerance.
    b. milk intolerance.
    c. milk allergy.
    d. lactose maldigestion.

21. The term for gastrointestinal symptoms resulting from the consumption of more lactose than can be digested with available lactase is called:
    a. lactose intolerance.
    b. milk intolerance.
    c. milk allergy.
    d. lactose maldigestion.

22. All of the following are true regarding MSG EXCEPT:
    a. in sensitive people it causes sweating, flushing, and rapid heartbeat.
    b. it should be avoided by everyone and removed from the market.
    c. it is a flavor enhancer.
    d. sensitivity is also known as "Chinese restaurant syndrome."

23. All of the following are true regarding celiac disease EXCEPT:
    a. it is an allergy to gluten, which is found in wheat, barley, rye, and triticale.
    b. the immune system reaction is localized to the small intestine.
    c. the rate of confirmed diagnosis is increasing in the U.S.
    d. the symptoms are easy to identify.

24. Which of the following groups of people experience food allergies most often?
    a. Older adults
    b. Young women
    c. Teen boys
    d. Infants and young children

25. In order to prevent allergic reactions in infants and young children, which food should NOT be given during the first year of life?
    a. Potatoes
    b. Bananas
    c. Grapes
    d. Cow's milk

26. People experience adverse reactions to food for all of the following reasons EXCEPT:
    a. food poisoning.
    b. aversion to the taste.
    c. food allergy.
    d. food intolerance.

27. "Gastrointestinal upsets" refers to all of the following EXCEPT:
    a. diarrhea.
    b. vomiting.
    c. congestion.
    d. cramps.

28. The only treatment available for food allergies is:
    a. eating smaller portions of the food.
    b. allergy shots.
    c. eliminating the food from the diet.
    d. allergy pills.

29. Symptoms of lactose intolerance include which of the following?
    a. Skin rash
    b. Hives
    c. Asthma
    d. Flatulence

30. Foods that contain low amounts of lactose that can generally be consumed in significant quantities by lactose-intolerant individuals include all of the following EXCEPT:
   a. hard cheese.
   b. milk.
   c. buttermilk.
   d yogurt.

To check yourself, use the answer key at the bottom of the page.[18]

---

[18] 1. c, 2. d, 3. d, 4. b, 5. c, 6. c, 7. a, 8. c, 9. c, 10. c, 11. a, 12. b, 13. b, 14. a, 15. d, 16. a, 17. b, 18. d, 19. d, 20. d, 21. a, 22. b, 23. d, 24. d, 25. d, 26. b, 27. c, 28. c, 29. d, 30. b

Unit 18 – Fats and Cholesterol in Health

Key Concepts

- Fats are our most concentrated source of food energy. They supply 9 calories per gram.
- Dietary fats "carry" the essential fatty acids, fat-soluble vitamins, and healthful phytochemicals along with them in foods.
- Fats are not created equal. Some types of fat have positive effects, and some have negative effects on health.
- Saturated fats and *trans* fats raise blood cholesterol levels more than does dietary cholesterol or any other type of fat.

Unit Outline

I. Changing views about fat intake and health
II. Facts about fats
   A. Functions of dietary fats
      1. Fats in foods supply energy and fat-soluble nutrients
      2. Fat contributes to the body's energy stores
      3. Fats increase the flavor and palatability of foods
      4. Fats contribute to the sensation of feeling full
      5. Fats are a component of cell membranes, vitamin D, and sex hormones
III. Fats come in many varieties
   A. Saturated and unsaturated fats
   B. The omega-6 and omega-3 fatty acids
      1. EPA and DHA
      2. Increasing omega-3 fatty acid intake
         a. EPA- and DHA-fortified foods
   C. Hydrogenated fats
      1. What's hydrogenation?
      2. *Trans* fatty acids
IV. Checking out cholesterol
   A. Sources of cholesterol
   B. The contributions of cholesterol
V. Finding out about the fat content of food
   A. Fat labeling
   B. Recent changes in recommendations for fat and cholesterol intake
      1. "Good" fats, "bad" fats
VII. Recommendations for fat and cholesterol intake

Unit Glossary

- **lipids:** Compounds that are insoluble in water and soluble in fat. Triglycerides, saturated and unsaturated fats, and essential fatty acids are examples of lipids, or "fats."
- **essential fatty acids:** Components of fats (linoleic acid, pronounced lynn-oh-lay-ick, and alpha-linolenic acid, pronounced lynn-oh-len-ick) required in the diet.
- **triglycerides:** Fats in which the glycerol molecule has three fatty acids attached to it; also called triacylglycerol. Triglycerides are the most common type of fat in foods and in body fat stores.
- **saturated fats:** Molecules of fat in which adjacent carbons within fatty acids are linked only by single bonds. The carbons are "saturated" with hydrogens; that is, they are attached to the maximum

possible number of hydrogens. Saturated fats tend to be solid at room temperature. Animal products and palm and coconut oil are sources of saturated fats.

- **unsaturated fats:** Molecules of fat in which adjacent carbons are linked by one or more double bonds. The carbons are not saturated with hydrogens; that is, they are attached to fewer than the maximum possible number of hydrogens. Unsaturated fats tend to be liquid at room temperature and are found in plants, vegetable oils, meats, and dairy products.
- **glycerol:** A syrupy, colorless liquid component of fats that is soluble in water. It is similar to glucose in chemical structure.
- **cholesterol:** A fat-soluble, colorless liquid found in animals but not in plants. Cholesterol is used by the body to form hormones such as testosterone and estrogen and is a component of animal cell membranes.
- **diglyceride:** A fat in which the glycerol molecule has two fatty acids attached to it; also called diacylglycerol.
- **monoglyceride:** A fat in which the glycerol molecule has one fatty acid attached to it; also called monoacylglycerol.
- **monounsaturated fats:** Fats that contain a fatty acid in which one carbon-carbon bond is not saturated with hydrogen.
- **polyunsaturated fats:** Fats that contain a fatty acid in which two or more carbon–carbon bonds are not saturated with hydrogen.
- **hydrogenation:** The addition of hydrogen to unsaturated fatty acids.
- *trans* **fats:** Unsaturated fatty acids in fats that contain atoms of hydrogen attached to opposite sides of carbons joined by a double bond.

Practice Multiple-Choice Test

1. All of the following are roles that dietary fats play EXCEPT:
    a. they serve as a source of concentrated energy.
    b. they increase the flavor and palatability of foods.
    c. they are used to replace red blood cells.
    d. they carry the fat-soluble vitamins.

2. The structure of a triglyceride is:
    a. 1 fatty acid and a glycerol.
    b. 2 fatty acids and a glycerol.
    c. 3 fatty acids and a glycerol.
    d. 4 fatty acids and a glycerol.

3. All of the following describe unsaturated fatty acids EXCEPT:
    a. they have one or more double bonds.
    b. they tend to be liquid at room temperature.
    c. plant foods are the best sources.
    d. monounsaturated fats have two double bonds.

4. Good sources of monounsaturated fats include all of the following EXCEPT:
    a. canola oil.
    b. olive oil.
    c. coconut oil.
    d. soybean oil.

5. Foods that contain the highest percentage of saturated fatty acids include all of the following EXCEPT:
   a. nuts and seeds.
   b. meats.
   c. cheese.
   d. whole milk.

6. Among the following, the newest addition to the Nutrition Facts panel is:
   a. *trans* fat.
   b. saturated fats.
   c. fiber.
   d. net carbs.

7. Which of the following is a drawback of the process of hydrogenation?
   a. Extended shelf life in foods
   b. Increased percentage of saturated fats
   c. Changes in cooking properties
   d. Changes in taste

8. All of the following are true regarding cholesterol EXCEPT:
   a. it is only found in animal products.
   b. two-thirds of the cholesterol in the body is produced by the liver.
   c. it is an essential nutrient.
   d. one-third of the cholesterol in the body comes from dietary sources.

9. Good sources of healthy fats include all of the following EXCEPT:
   a. fish and seafood.
   b. vegetable oils.
   c. bakery foods.
   d. walnuts.

10. Sources of unhealthy fats include all of the following EXCEPT:
    a. eggs.
    b. snack foods.
    c. steak.
    d. nuts.

11. Lipids provide:
    a. 9 calories per gram.
    b. 7 calories per gram.
    c. 5 calories per gram.
    d. 4 calories per gram.

12. In the body, fats serve as a component of all of the following EXCEPT:
    a. cell membranes.
    b. vitamin D.
    c. sex hormones.
    d. enzymes.

13. Compounds that are insoluble in water and soluble in fat are:
    a. carbohydrates.
    b. lipids.
    c. proteins.
    d. vitamins.

14. The class of compounds known as lipids includes all of the following EXCEPT:
    a. triglycerides.
    b. monosaccharides.
    c. saturated fats.
    d. essential fatty acids.

15. Fats that are required in the diet are:
    a. functional fatty acids.
    b. necessary fatty acids.
    c. essential fatty acids.
    d. saturated fatty acids.

16. Triglycerides make up _____ of dietary fat and the majority of body fat stores.
    a. 98%
    b. 75%
    c. 50%
    d. 25%

17. All of the following describe saturated fatty acids EXCEPT:
    a. they tend to be solid at room temperature.
    b. animal products are rich in saturated fats.
    c. they have one or more double bonds.
    d. they promote heart disease.

18. All of the following are true regarding omega-3 and omega-6 fatty acids EXCEPT:
    a. they must be included in the diet.
    b. certain ones are called essential fatty acids.
    c. they are found in plant and animal foods.
    d. they are both monounsaturated fats.

19. The addition of hydrogen atoms to unsaturated fatty acids is called:
    a. cholesterol.
    b. hydrogenation.
    c. stabilization.
    d. saturation.

20. Unsaturated fatty acids that contain atoms of hydrogen attached to the opposite sides of carbons joined by a double bond are:
    a. *cis* fatty acids.
    b. *trans* fatty acids.
    c. sterols.
    d. linoleic acids.

98

21. The most common naturally occurring form of unsaturated fatty acids that contain hydrogens located on the same side of the double bond are:
    a. *cis* fatty acids.
    b. *trans* fatty acids.
    c. sterols.
    d. linoleic acids.

22. The body uses cholesterol for all of the following EXCEPT:
    a. to produce estrogen.
    b. to produce testosterone.
    c. as a concentrated source of energy.
    d. as a component of nerves.

23. If a granola bar weighs 35 grams, provides 140 calories, and contains 4.5 grams of total fat, what percentage of its calories come from fat?
    a. 25%
    b. 4%
    c. 41%
    d. 29%

24. A "reduced cholesterol" product must contain:
    a. 20 milligrams or less per serving.
    b. 50% less cholesterol than normal.
    c. 40 milligrams or less per serving.
    d. 75% less cholesterol than normal.

25. Current recommendations for adults are to consume _____ of total calories from fat:
    a. 15% to 20%
    b. 20% to 35%
    c. 30% to 40%
    d. <15%

26. The Adequate Intake for linoleic acid for men is:
    a. 12 grams.
    b. 15 grams.
    c. 17 grams.
    d. 20 grams.

27. The Adequate Intake for linoleic acid for women is:
    a. 12 grams.
    b. 15 grams.
    c. 17 grams.
    d. 20 grams.

28. Consumption of two fish meals per week reduces the risk of all of the following EXCEPT:
    a. heart attack.
    b. heart disease.
    c. stroke.
    d. cirrhosis.

29. Good sources of omega-3 fatty acids include all of the following EXCEPT:
    a. sardines.
    b. cheese.
    c. mackerel.
    d. salmon.

30. EPA and DHA are found in all of the following EXCEPT:
    a. oysters.
    b. shrimp.
    c. legumes.
    d. halibut.

To check yourself, use the answer key at the bottom of the page.[19]

---

[19] 1. c, 2. c, 3. d, 4. c, 5. a, 6. a, 7. b, 8. c, 9. c, 10. d, 11. a, 12. d, 13. b, 14. b, 15. c, 16. a, 17. c, 18. d, 19. b, 20. b, 21. a, 22. c, 23. d, 24. d, 25. b, 26. c, 27. a, 28. d, 29. b, 30. c

Unit 19 – Nutrition and Heart Disease

Key Concepts

- Heart disease is the leading cause of death in men and women in the United States.
- Disease, dietary and lifestyle factors are among the most important contributors to heart disease.
- Moderate-fat diets that provide primarily "healthy fats" decrease heart disease risk to a greater extent than do low-fat, high-carbohydrate diets.
- Lowering high blood LDL-cholesterol and raising HDL-cholesterol levels reduces the risk of heart disease.

Unit Outline

I.   The diet-heart disease connection
    A.   Declining rates of heart disease
II. A primer on heart disease
    A.   What is heart disease?
    B.   What causes atherosclerosis?
        1.   Blood cholesterol levels and heart disease
        2.   All blood cholesterol is not equal
            a.   Understanding HDL and LDL
            b.   Triglycerides and heart disease risk
            c.   Genetic effects on blood cholesterol levels
        3.   Chronic inflammation and heart disease
III. Who's at risk for heart disease?
    A.   Are the risks the same for women as for men?
IV. Diet and lifestyle in the management of heart disease
    A.   Modification of blood lipid levels
    B.   Modification of chronic inflammation and oxidation
    C.   The statins
V.   Looking toward the future

Unit Glossary

- **heart disease:** One of a number of disorders that result when circulation of blood to parts of the heart is inadequate. Also called coronary heart disease. ("Coronary" refers to the blood vessels at the top of the heart. They look somewhat like a crown.)
- **plaque:** Deposits of cholesterol, other fats, calcium, and cell materials in the lining of the inner wall of arteries.
- **atherosclerosis:** "Hardening of the arteries" due to a buildup of plaque.
- **cardiovascular disease:** Disorders related to plaque buildup in arteries of the heart, brain, and other organs and tissues.
- **chronic inflammation:** Inflammation that lasts weeks, months, or years. Inflammation is the first response of the body's immune system to infection or irritation. It triggers the release of biologically active substances that promote oxidation and other potentially harmful reactions in the body.
- **endothelium** (Pronounced n-dough-theil-e-um): The layer of cells lining the inside of blood vessels.
- **plant stanols and sterols:** Substances in corn, wheat, oats, rye, olives, wood, and some other plants that are similar in structure to cholesterol but that are not absorbed by the body. They decrease cholesterol absorption.

Practice Multiple-Choice Test

1. Since the 1950s, rates of heart disease have decreased 60% due to all of the following reasons EXCEPT:
    a. declines in blood cholesterol levels.
    b. decline in average body weights.
    c. reduced rates of smoking.
    d. advances in medications.

2. All of the following are true regarding heart disease EXCEPT:
    a. worldwide it accounts for 1 out of every 4 deaths.
    b. Caucasians have a higher risk than African Americans.
    c. men and women have equal risks for developing it.
    d. women die on average 10 years later than men from heart disease.

3. "Hardening of the arteries" due to build-up of plaque is called:
    a. stroke.
    b. calcification.
    c. endotheliosis.
    d. atherosclerosis.

4. A cluster of disorders resulting from inadequate circulation of blood to parts of the heart is called:
    a. high cholesterol.
    b. high blood pressure.
    c. stroke.
    d. heart disease.

5. All of the following are risk factors for heart disease EXCEPT:
    a. high HDL levels.
    b. high triglycerides.
    c. chronic inflammation.
    d. certain genetic traits.

6. All of the following are true regarding LDL cholesterol EXCEPT:
    a. dietary saturated fats increase LDL levels.
    b. it is also known as "bad" cholesterol.
    c. it carries less cholesterol than HDL.
    d. its cholesterol can be incorporated into plaque.

7. The layer of cells lining the inside of blood vessels is called the:
    a. cytoplasm.
    b. endometrium.
    c. endothelium.
    d. mitochondria.

8. Deposits of cholesterol, other fats, calcium, and cell materials in the lining of the inner wall of arteries are called:
    a. angina.
    b. lipoproteins.
    c. plaque.
    d. blockages.

102

9. All of the following contribute to the risk of heart attack EXCEPT:
   a. loss of body weight.
   b. physical inactivity.
   c. smoking.
   d. hypertension.

10. Substances in certain foods such as oats and olives that are similar in structure to cholesterol but that are not absorbed by the body and act to decrease cholesterol absorption are called:
    a. *trans* fats and functional fats.
    b. phytochemicals.
    c. stanols and sterols.
    d. steroids.

11. Another term for heart disease is:
    a. coronary heart disease.
    b. atherosclerosis.
    c. plaque.
    d. pulmonary disease.

12. Disorders related to plaque buildup in arteries of the heart, brain, and other organs and tissues are called:
    a. atherosclerosis.
    b. cardiovascular disease.
    c. hypertension.
    d. embolisms.

13. All of the following are characteristics of angina EXCEPT:
    a. it occurs when arteries are narrowed by 50% or more.
    b. it is due to a shortage of blood flow to the heart.
    c. it can result in pain that is felt in the chest.
    d. it only occurs in people over age 55.

14. Which of the following conditions are known to increase plaque formation in arteries?
    a. High HDL cholesterol and high blood pressure
    b. High HDL cholesterol and chronic inflammation
    c. High total cholesterol and chronic inflammation
    d. High HDL cholesterol and high triglycerides

15. All of the following are true regarding HDL cholesterol EXCEPT:
    a. it is also known as "good" cholesterol.
    b. it helps remove cholesterol from the blood.
    c. high HDL is protective against heart disease.
    d. increasing sources of dietary polyunsaturated fats raises HDL levels.

16. All of the following contribute to increased blood cholesterol levels EXCEPT:
    a. *trans* fats.
    b. smoking.
    c. saturated fats.
    d. physical activity.

103

17. Nutrients and substances that reduce chronic inflammation include all of the following EXCEPT:
    a. EPA and DHA.
    b. vitamin D.
    c. nuts, tea, fruits, vegetables, and whole grains.
    d. calcium and magnesium.

18. Leading risk factors for heart disease include all of the following EXCEPT:
    a. smoking.
    b. diabetes.
    c. age over 40 in men, or over 45 in women.
    d. a diet low in fruits, vegetables, and whole grains.

19. Examples of substances that contain stanols include all of the following EXCEPT:
    a. corn.
    b. olives.
    c. oats.
    d. okra.

20. All of the following dietary factors decrease LDL cholesterol EXCEPT:
    a. mono- and polyunsaturated fats.
    b. *trans* fats.
    c. whole-grain products.
    d. nuts.

21. All of the following lifestyle and dietary factors increase HDL cholesterol EXCEPT:
    a. moderate fat intake.
    b. physical activity.
    c. alcohol.
    d. polyunsaturated fats.

22. Triglyceride levels can be decreased by incorporating all of the following lifestyle and dietary factors EXCEPT:
    a. moderate-fat diets.
    b. high-carbohydrate diets.
    c. DHA and EPA.
    d. physical activity.

23. All of the following are characteristics of diets that lower heart-disease risk EXCEPT:
    a. provide 35-40% of total calories from fat.
    b. emphasize healthy fats.
    c. are high in fiber: 35 grams per day for men, or 25 grams per day for women.
    d. are moderate in fats and contain limited amounts of sugars.

24. Food choices that promote health and lower heart-disease risk include all of the following EXCEPT:
    a. nuts.
    b. olive, peanut, and flaxseed oils.
    c. full-fat dairy products.
    d. fish.

25. All of the following are true regarding statins EXCEPT:
    a. use results in a 30% drop in LDL cholesterol, and a 30-40% reduction in heart attack and stroke.
    b. they are inexpensive.
    c. they have side effects such as liver disease and kidney failure.
    d. they act by reducing cholesterol production in the liver.

26. The "portfolio diet" is
    a. an extreme cholesterol-lowering diet.
    b. a low-carbohydrate diet.
    c. a diet for lowering blood pressure.
    d. a diet for reversing aging.

27. All of the following are true regarding the portfolio diet EXCEPT:
    a. it is a vegetarian diet.
    b. it is based on soy-based foods.
    c. the diet reduces cholesterol as much as statins.
    d. it is not much different from the typical U.S. diet.

28. All of the following are true regarding heart disease EXCEPT:
    a. heart disease develops slowly over time.
    b. heart disease is a chronic disease.
    c. heart disease results from narrowing of the arteries due to plaque build-up.
    d. a diet high in monounsaturated fats increases heart disease risk.

29. All of the following are true regarding chronic inflammation EXCEPT:
    a. it lasts for weeks, months, or years.
    b. it triggers the release of substances that promote oxidation.
    c. it is interrelated with high blood cholesterol levels.
    d. there is no way to treat it.

30. Total cholesterol readings are a combination of which of the following levels?
    a. HDL and triglycerides
    b. HDL and LDL
    c. LDL and proteins
    d. HDL and phospholipids

To check yourself, use the answer key at the bottom of the page.[20]

---

[20] 1. b, 2. b, 3. d, 4. d, 5. a, 6. c, 7. c, 8. c, 9. a, 10. c, 11. a, 12. b, 13. d, 14. c, 15. d, 16. d, 17. d, 18. c, 19. c, 20. b, 21. d, 22. b, 23. a, 24. c, 25. b, 26. a, 27. d, 28. d, 29. d, 30. b

Unit 20 – Vitamins and Your Health

Key Concepts

- Vitamins are chemical substances found in food that are required for normal growth and health.
- Adequate intakes of vitamins protect people against deficiency diseases and help prevent a number of chronic diseases and disorders.
- Each vitamin has a range of intake in which it functions optimally. Intakes below and above the range impair health.
- Eating five or more servings of fruits and vegetables each day is a good way to get enough vitamins in your diet.

Unit Outline

I.   Vitamins: they're on center stage
    A. Vitamin facts
        1. Water- and fat-soluble vitamins
        2. Bogus vitamins
    B. What do vitamins do?
    C. Protection from vitamin deficiencies and more
        1. Folate, neural tube defects, dementia, and cancer
        2. Vitamin A—from measles to "liver spots"
        3. Vitamin D: From osteoporosis to chronic inflammation
            a. Recommended intake of vitamin D
            b. The sun as a source of vitamin D
        4. Vitamin C and the common cold revisited
    D. The antioxidant vitamins
II. Vitamins: getting enough without getting too much
    A. Preserving the vitamin content of foods
        1. Recommended intake levels of vitamins

Unit Glossary

- **vitamins:** Chemical substances that perform specific functions in the body.
- **coenzymes:** Chemical substances, including many vitamins, that activate specific enzymes. Activated enzymes increase the rate at which reactions take place in the body, such as the breakdown of fats or carbohydrates in the small intestine and the conversion of glucose and fatty acids into energy within cells.
- **dementia** (Pronounced di-men-cha.): A usually progressive condition (such as Alzheimer's disease) marked by the development of memory impairment and an inability to use or comprehend words or to plan and initiate complex behaviors.
- **chronic inflammation:** Low grade inflammation that lasts weeks, months, or years. Inflammation is the first response of the body's immune system to infection or irritation. Inflammation triggers the release of biologically active substances that promote oxidation and other potentially harmful reactions in the body.
- **antioxidants:** Chemical substances that prevent or repair damage to cells caused by exposure to free radicals. Beta-carotene, vitamin E, and vitamin C function as antioxidants.
- **precursor:** In nutrition, a nutrient that can be converted into another nutrient (also called provitamin). Beta-carotene is a precursor of vitamin A.

106

- **free radicals:** Chemical substances (usually oxygen or hydrogen) that are missing an electron. The absence of the electron makes the chemical substances reactive and prone to oxidizing nearby atoms or molecules by stealing an electron from them.

Practice Multiple-Choice Test

1. A deficiency disease that results from inadequate intake of thiamin is called:
   a. pellagra.
   b. beriberi.
   c. spina bifida.
   d. rickets.

2. All of the following are true regarding vitamin A EXCEPT:
   a. beta-carotene serves as a precursor.
   b. deficiency is the leading cause of blindness in developing countries.
   c. it is highly toxic when consumed in excess.
   d. it is only found in plant sources.

3. All of the following are true regarding vitamin K EXCEPT:
   a. deficiency is widespread.
   b. it is an essential component of the body's clotting mechanism.
   c. it is produced by bacteria in the gut.
   d. leafy green vegetables are a good source.

4. All of the following are considered non-vitamins EXCEPT:
   a. rutin.
   b. pantothenic acid.
   c. bioflavinoids.
   d. inositol.

5. Since 1998, grain products have been fortified with which vitamin in an effort to reduce the incidence of neural tube defects?
   a. Calcium
   b. Folic acid
   c. Vitamin A
   d. Biotin

6. All of the following are true regarding vitamin D EXCEPT:
   a. deficiency in childhood results in rickets.
   b. exposure to sunlight allows the body to manufacture it.
   c. poor vitamin D status has only been reported in children.
   d. good sources include fortified milk and margarine.

7. All of the following are true regarding riboflavin EXCEPT:
   a. it is destroyed by exposure to light.
   b. good sources include milk, yogurt, and cheese.
   c. it is toxic in high amounts.
   d. it assists the body in the release and use of energy from the macronutrients.

8. All of the following are true regarding vitamin B_{12} EXCEPT:
   a. it is only found in plant sources.
   b. it is needed for normal red blood cell development.
   c. there are no known toxicity symptoms.
   d. deficiency results in pernicious anemia and neurological damage.

9. Which of the following is considered a precursor to a vitamin A?
   a. Bioflavinoids
   b. Biotin
   c. Beta-carotene
   d. Beriberi

10. Chemical substances that perform specific functions in the body, such as serving as coenzymes, are called:
    a. carbohydrates.
    b. proteins.
    c. vitamins.
    d. water.

11. Vitamins provide:
    a. 9 calories per gram.
    b. 7 calories per gram.
    c. 4 calories per gram.
    d. Vitamins do not provide calories.

12. All of the following are true regarding vitamins EXCEPT:
    a. fourteen have been discovered so far.
    b. they are considered nonessential nutrients.
    c. some dissolve in water and some in fat.
    d. they perform specific functions in the body.

13. All of the following are classified as fat-soluble vitamins EXCEPT:
    a. biotin.
    b. vitamin A.
    c. vitamin D.
    d. vitamin E.

14. All of the following are classified as water-soluble vitamins EXCEPT:
    a. vitamin C.
    b. thiamin.
    c. vitamin K.
    d. riboflavin.

15. Chemical substances that activate enzymes and assist in the conversion of the macronutrients into energy are called:
    a. hormones.
    b. provitamins.
    c. coenzymes.
    d. precursors.

108

16. Adequate intake of folate reduces the risk for all of the following EXCEPT:
    a. neural tube defects.
    b. dementia.
    c. osteoporosis.
    d. certain types of cancer.

17. A condition marked by the development of memory impairment and an inability to use or comprehend words or plan complex behavior is called:
    a. spina bifida.
    b. pellagra.
    c. dementia.
    d. beriberi.

18. All of the following vitamins are known to function as antioxidants EXCEPT:
    a. biotin.
    b. beta-carotene.
    c. vitamin E.
    d. vitamin C.

19. Another name for a provitamin, a nutrient that can be converted into another nutrient, is:
    a. coenzyme.
    b. precursor.
    c. predecessor.
    d. antioxidant.

20. Chemical substances that are missing an electron and are prone to oxidizing nearby atoms are called:
    a. antioxidants.
    b. provitamins.
    c. precursors.
    d. free radicals.

21. All of the following are true regarding vitamins EXCEPT:
    a. they are considered essential because the body cannot produce them.
    b. if adequate amounts are not consumed, deficiency diseases develop.
    c. they perform specific functions in the body.
    d. eating at least one serving of fruit or vegetable a day prevents deficiencies.

22. All of the following are true regarding fat-soluble vitamins EXCEPT:
    a. they are stored in body fat, the liver, and other parts of the body.
    b. deficiency symptoms take longer to develop than those associated with water-soluble vitamins.
    c. they can be highly toxic if consumed in excess.
    d. they include vitamins A, C, D, E, and K.

23. All of the following are true regarding water-soluble vitamins EXCEPT:
    a. excess amounts are usually excreted in the urine.
    b. they are stored in body fat, the liver, and other parts of the body.
    c. deficiency symptoms develop within weeks or months.
    d. they include the B-complex vitamins and vitamin C.

24. All of the following are true regarding niacin EXCEPT:
    a. a deficiency results in pellagra.
    b. its precursor is tryptophan.
    c. high doses result in flushing.
    d. high doses lower HDL-cholesterol levels.

25. All of the following are true regarding vitamin B$_6$ EXCEPT:
    a. it is needed for the conversion of trytophan to niacin.
    b. it is needed for normal red blood cell formation.
    c. toxicity symptoms include loss of feeling in fingers and toes.
    d. it is stored in the liver.

26. All of the following are true regarding folate EXCEPT:
    a. in pregnancy, deficiency can result in neural tube defects.
    b. deficiency results in elevated blood levels of homocysteine.
    c. the RDA for men and women is 200 mcg per day.
    d. fortified grain products are a good source.

27. All of the following are true regarding vitamin C EXCEPT:
    a. it acts as an antioxidant.
    b. it enhances iron absorption.
    c. deficiency results in spina bifida.
    d. it is important in the manufacture of collagen and wound healing.

28. All of the following are true regarding vitamin E EXCEPT:
    a. it acts as an antioxidant.
    b. it increases the ability of LDL cholesterol to form plaque in arteries.
    c. salad dressings are a good source.
    d. it is destroyed by exposure to oxygen and heat.

29. The best way to obtain adequate amounts of vitamins is:
    a. by taking supplements.
    b. by drinking protein shakes.
    c. by eating at least 5 to 9 servings of fruits and vegetables per day.
    d. by eating a low-carbohydrate diet.

30. All of the following are true regarding biotin EXCEPT:
    a. deficiency may results from overconsumption of raw eggs.
    b. excesses are rapidly excreted.
    c. it has no known functions.
    d. good sources are meats, eggs, and cereal grains.

To check yourself, use the answer key at the bottom of the page.[21]

---

[21] 1. b, 2. d, 3. a, 4. b, 5. b, 6. c, 7. c, 8. a, 9. c, 10. c, 11. d, 12. b, 13. a, 14. c, 15. c, 16. c, 17. c, 18. a, 19. b, 20. d, 21. d, 22. d, 23. b, 24. d, 25. d, 26. c, 27. c, 28. b, 29. c, 30. c

Unit 21 – Phytochemicals and Genetically Modified Food

Key Concepts

- Plants contain thousands of substances in addition to essential nutrients that affect body processes and health.
- Diets containing lots of vegetables, fruits, whole grains, and other plant foods are strongly associated with the prevention of chronic diseases such as heart disease and cancer.
- Biotechnology is rapidly changing the characteristics and types of foods available to consumers.
- Not all substances that occur naturally in foods are safe to eat.

Unit Outline

I.   Phytochemicals: Nutrition superstars
   A. Characteristics of phytochemicals
   B. Phytochemicals and health
   C. Phytochemicals work in groups
      1. The case of beta-carotene supplements
      2. Vegetable extracts and essences
   D. How do phytochemicals work?
   E. Diets high in plant foods
   F. Naturally occurring toxins in food
      1. Beware of ackee fruit
      2. What's the scoop on caffeine?
II. Genetically modified foods
   A. Genetic modification of animals
      1. Animal clones
   B. GM foods: Are they safe and acceptable?

Unit Glossary

- **phytochemicals** (phyto = plant): Chemical substances in plants, some of which perform important functions in the body.
- **zoochemicals:** Chemical substances in animal foods, some of which likely perform important functions in the body.
- **phytochemicals** (phyto = plant): Chemical substances in plants, some of which perform important functions in the body.
- **zoochemicals:** Chemical substances in animal foods, some of which likely perform important functions in the body.
- **cruciferous vegetables:** Sulfur-containing vegetables whose outer leaves form a cross (or crucifix). Vegetables in this family include broccoli, cabbage, cauliflower, brussels sprouts, mustard and collard greens, kale, bok choy, kohlrabi, rutabaga, turnips, broccoflower, and watercress.
- **biotechnology:** As applied to food products, the process of modifying the composition of foods by biologically altering their genetic makeup. Also called genetic engineering of foods. The food products produced are sometimes referred to as "GM" and GMOs (genetically modified organisms).

Practice Multiple-Choice Test

1. Phytochemicals serve all of the following functions in plants EXCEPT:
   a. they provide color.
   b. they protect plants from insects, microbes, and oxidation due to exposure to sunlight.
   c. all phytochemicals are beneficial to health.
   d. the amount and type present in plants may vary a great deal.

2. Chemical substances in plants, some of which perform important functions in the body, are called:
   a. zoochemicals.
   b. antioxidants.
   c. phytochemicals.
   d. free radicals.

3. All of the following are true regarding phytochemicals EXCEPT:
   a. there are thousands of them in plants.
   b. they are considered essential nutrients.
   c. the body cannot make them.
   d. they are not easily destroyed by cooking or storage.

4. All of the following are true regarding age-related macular degeneration EXCEPT:
   a. it is caused by oxidation of the central portion of the eye.
   b. it is the leading cause of blindness in U.S. adults over the age of 65.
   c. antioxidants provided by carotenoids in dark green, leafy vegetables may help prevent it.
   d. cause-and-effect studies have proven that high phytochemical intake is preventative.

5. Which of the following is true regarding phytochemicals?
   a. Supplements have the same benefits as consuming the whole foods.
   b. They work individually.
   c. Absorption depends on the presence of other phytochemicals and nutrients in foods.
   d. The optimal combinations of different types are known.

6. Sulfur-containing phytochemicals found in cruciferous vegetables that increase the body's ability to neutralize cancer-causing substances are called:
   a. indoles.
   b. allicins.
   c. terpenes.
   d. phytoestrogens.

7. Top sources of foods with the highest concentration of antioxidants in a typical serving include all of the following EXCEPT:
   a. blackberries.
   b. soy nuts.
   c. strawberries.
   d. blueberries.

8. All of the following are true EXCEPT:
   a. caffeine is a phytochemical.
   b. too much caffeine causes sleeplessness.
   c. habitual consumption of coffee appears to decrease the risk of cardiovascular disease.
   d. the beneficial effects of coffee appear to be related to the caffeine content.

112

9. All of the following are true regarding biotechnology EXCEPT:
   a. the products are referred to as "GM" and "GMOs."
   b. it is the process of modifying the composition of foods by altering their genetic makeup.
   c. it is also called genetic engineering.
   d. biotechnology is only used in plants, not in animals.

10. Chemical substances in animal foods, some of which perform important functions in the body, are called:
    a. zoochemicals.
    b. antioxidants.
    c. phytochemicals.
    d. free radicals.

11. All of the following are true regarding phytochemicals EXCEPT:
    a. they are excreted within a day or two, making consistent intake important.
    b. cooking vegetables or consuming with small amounts of fats increases absorption.
    c. some foods contain hundreds of phytochemicals.
    d. they serve as precursors to free radical formation.

12. Phytochemicals are associated with reduced risk of developing all of the following diseases EXCEPT
    a. heart disease.
    b. type 1 diabetes.
    c. cataracts.
    d. certain types of cancers.

13. Sulfur-containing vegetables include which of the following?
    a. Broccoli and cabbage
    b. Zucchini and squash
    c. Onions and garlic
    d. Carrots and peas

14. Roles that phytochemicals play in disease reduction include all of the following EXCEPT:
    a. decreasing formation of blood clots.
    b. blocking or neutralizing enzymes that promote the development of cancer.
    c. acting as hormone-initiating substances in cancer.
    d. serving as antioxidants that prevent and repair damage to cells due to oxidation.

15. A phytochemical in spinach that can cause stomachaches is called:
    a. solanine.
    b. phytates.
    c. oxalic acid.
    d. folic acid.

16. A naturally occurring substance in whole grains that can make certain minerals unavailable for absorption is called:
    a. solanine.
    b. phytates.
    c. oxalic acid.
    d. cyanide.

17. A disease caused by an overdose of the naturally occurring toxin cyanide in cassava root is called:
    a. ackee.
    b. cataracts.
    c. cyanosis.
    d. konzo.

18. Real and potential benefits related to GM crops and foods include all of the following EXCEPT:
    a. GM crops may cross-pollinate with local crops and reduce the market for locally grown foods.
    b. increased crop yield.
    c. improved food flavors.
    d. reduced herbicide and pesticide use.

19. Real and potential concerns related to GM crops and foods include all of the following EXCEPT:
    a. foods produced may be unacceptable to consumers.
    b. decreased waste due to spoilage.
    c. long-term effects of GM organisms on local plants and insects are unknown.
    d. Europe does not allow the importation of GM foods.

20. Which of the following has the highest caffeine content?
    a. Excedrin
    b. Chocolate milk
    c. Coca-Cola
    d. Green tea

21. All of the following are true regarding genetic modification of animals EXCEPT:
    a. salmon have been engineered to grow faster.
    b. cattle have been engineered to have leaner muscles.
    c. genetically engineered animals must be labeled as such when sold for food.
    d. pigs have been engineered to produce less smelly stools and gas.

22. Phytochemicals found in edible and nonedible oils that have been shown to decrease blood LDL-cholesterol levels are called:
    a. carotenoids.
    b. plant stanols and sterols.
    c. lignans.
    d. terpenes.

23. Phytochemicals found in dark green vegetables and orange and yellow vegetables that can decrease the development of macular degeneration are called:
    a. phytoestrogens.
    b. allicins.
    c. carotenoids.
    d. flavonoids.

24. Phytochemicals that have been shown to increase HDL-cholesterol and decrease plaque formation and that are found in red wine and chocolate are called:
    a. flavonoids.
    b. carotenoids.
    c. saponins.
    d. indoles.

114

25. Phytochemicals that are found in soy foods that lower cholesterol and decrease menopausal symptoms are called:
    a. indoles.
    b. allicins.
    c. plant stanols.
    d. phytoestrogens.

26. A phytochemical that is found in garlic and onions that decreases the production of cholesterol by the liver is called:
    a. terpene.
    b. allicin.
    c. lignan.
    d. beta-carotene.

27. Phytochemicals that are found in oranges, lemons, and grapefruits that facilitate the excretion of cancer-causing substances are called:
    a. flavonoids.
    b. allicins.
    c. indoles.
    d. terpenes.

28. Phytochemicals that interfere with the action of estrogen that are found in flaxseed and soybeans are called:
    a. saponins.
    b. carotinoids.
    c. lignans.
    d. indoles.

29. Phytochemicals that are found in high amounts in dried beans and that neutralize cancer-causing enzymes in the gut are called:
    a. plant stanols.
    b. sterols.
    c. lignans.
    d. saponins.

30. All of the following are true regarding flavonoids EXCEPT:
    a. they were originally called "vitamin P."
    b. over 4000 have been identified.
    c. they give red wines and dark teas a bitter taste.
    d. they decrease HDL-cholesterol.

To check yourself, use the answer key at the bottom of the page.[22]

---

[22] 1. c, 2. c, 3. b, 4. d, 5. c, 6. a, 7. b, 8. d, 9. d, 10. a, 11. d, 12. b, 13. a, 14. c, 15. c, 16. b, 17. d, 18. a, 19. b, 20. a, 21. c, 22. b, 23. c, 24. a, 25. d, 26. b, 27. d, 28. c, 29. d, 30. d

Unit 22 – Diet and Cancer

Key Concepts

- Cancer has many different causes. Diet is a major factor that influences the development of most types of cancer.
- Diets primarily based on plant foods that include lean meats, fish, and low-fat dairy products; regular physical activity; and normal levels of body fat reduce cancer risk.
- Cancer is largely preventable, but there are no absolute guarantees that an individual will not develop cancer.

Unit Outline

I. What is cancer?
   A. How does cancer develop?
   B. What causes cancer?
II. Fighting cancer with a fork
   A. Dietary risk factors for cancer: A closer look
      1. Fruits and vegetables and cancer
      2. Color-coding vegetable and fruit choices
      3. Whole grains and cancer
      4. Saturated fat and cancer prevention
      5. Nitrate-preserved and grilled meats and cancer
   B. Diet and cancer guidelines
      1. Alcohol intake and cancer
      2. Excess body fat and cancer
   C. Bogus cancer treatments
   D. Eating to beat the odds

Unit Glossary

- **cancer:** A group of diseases in which abnormal cells grow out of control and can spread throughout the body. Cancer is not contagious and has many causes.
- **prostate:** A gland located above the testicles in males. The prostate secretes a fluid that surrounds sperm.
- **initiation phase:** The start of the cancer process; it begins with the alteration of DNA within cells.
- **promotion phase:** The period in cancer development when the number of cells with altered DNA increases.
- **progression phase:** The period in cancer development when the cells with altered DNA grow uncontrollably and rapidly, until they are numerous enough to impair the functioning of surrounding tissues.

Practice Multiple-Choice Test

1. The most common sites for cancer development in the body include all of the following EXCEPT the:
   a. prostate.
   b. breast.
   c. stomach.
   d. colon.

2. The start of the cancer process that begins with the alteration of DNA within cells is called the:
   a. promotion phase.
   b. progression phase.
   c. remission phase.
   d. initiation phase.

3. The period in cancer development when the number of cells with altered DNA increases is called the:
   a. promotion phase.
   b. progression phase.
   c. remission phase.
   d. initiation phase.

4. Toxic substances that damage the DNA of cells leading to the initiation of cancer are generated by all of the following EXCEPT:
   a. tobacco smoke.
   b. obesity.
   c. high intake of fruits and vegetables.
   d. certain viruses.

5. Dietary patterns and lifestyles related to reduced risk of cancer and heart disease include all of the following EXCEPT:
   a. losing excess weight.
   b. including 20 minutes of physical activity 3 times a week.
   c. excluding charred meats.
   d. excluding smoking.

6. As vegetable and fruit intake increases (5+ servings per day), cancer incidence decreases due to all of the following EXCEPT:
   a. high intake of phytochemicals.
   b. high intake of vitamin C.
   c. high intake of vitamin E.
   d. high intake of magnesium.

7. All of the following are true regarding lycopene EXCEPT:
   a. it is found in red fruits and vegetables.
   b. it is a prooxidant.
   c. vegetable sources are tomatoes and peppers.
   d. fruit sources are red raspberries and strawberries.

8. Characteristics of cancer-promoting diets include all of the following EXCEPT:
   a. low intake of vegetables and fruits.
   b. low intake of whole grains, beans, and nuts.
   c. regular intake of charred and nitrate-cured meats.
   d. high intake of monounsaturated fats.

9. The second leading cause of death in the United States is:
   a. heart disease.
   b. diabetes.
   c. cancer.
   d. stroke.

10. A gland located above the testicles in males that is a common site of cancer development is the:
    a. lymph node.
    b. prostate.
    c. appendix.
    d. gallbladder.

11. All of the following are true regarding cancer EXCEPT:
    a. it is contagious.
    b. it results when abnormal cells grow out of control.
    c. cancerous cells can spread throughout the body.
    d. it has many causes.

12. All of the following may repair damage to cells and halt the progression of cancer EXCEPT:
    a. antioxidants.
    b. free radicals.
    c. protective mechanisms in the body.
    d. protective substances in foods.

13. Approximately what percentage of all cancers are related to environmental factors that modify the structure and function of DNA?
    a. 10%
    b. 25%
    c. 50-75%
    d. 80-90%

14. Diet accounts for approximately what percentage of cancer risk?
    a. 20%
    b. 30%
    c. 40%
    d. 50%

15. Characteristics of the promotion phase of cancer include all of the following EXCEPT:
    a. this phase takes place over a span of 5 to 7 years.
    b. large numbers of abnormal cells are produced during this phase.
    c. cells with altered DNA divide during this phase.
    d. unless corrected, it will lead to the progression phase.

16. The progression phase of cancer has all of the following characteristics EXCEPT:
    a. abnormal cells increase rapidly.
    b. the abnormal cells impair the normal functions of the tissue where they are growing.
    c. abnormal cells may migrate to other tissues and cause DNA damage.
    d. this phase is easily curable.

17. All of the following are environmental factors related to cancer development worldwide EXCEPT:
    a. physical inactivity.
    b. hepatitis A viral infection.
    c. excess alcohol intake.
    d. unsafe sex.

118

18. Research has shown that people who migrate from countries with low rates of cancer to those with high rates increase their cancer risk due to:
    a. difficulty learning the language.
    b. homesickness.
    c. Westernization of diet and lifestyle.
    d. difficulty "fitting in."

19. Having a genetic predisposition to cancer means:
    a. cancer may develop if you are regularly exposed to certain substances.
    b. there is a 100% certainty that cancer will develop.
    c. a genetic based susceptibility develops during adulthood.
    d. exposure to viruses during periods of slow growth can modify the function of genes.

20. All of the following are true regarding the genetic basis of cancer EXCEPT:
    a. genetic factors account for 42% of prostate cancers.
    b. genetic factors account for 5 to 27% of breast cancers.
    c. genetic factors account for 36% of pancreatic cancers.
    d. genetic factors account for 40% of bone cancers.

21. Diet recommendations for cancer reduction include all of the following EXCEPT:
    a. 5+ servings of vegetables and fruits daily.
    b. regular consumption of dried beans, nuts, and seeds.
    c. one serving of whole grains/products daily.
    d. eating foods that are low in saturated fat.

22. Frequent consumption of which of the following foods has been associated with decreased risk of prostate cancer?
    a. Dark chocolate
    b. Black and green teas
    c. Tomatoes and tomato products
    d. Oatmeal

23. Frequent consumption of which of the following foods has been associated with decreased risk of breast and ovarian cancer?
    a. Dark chocolate
    b. Black and green teas
    c. Tomatoes and tomato products
    d. Oatmeal

24. The cancer-protective components of whole grains include all of the following EXCEPT:
    a. fiber.
    b. unsaturated fatty acids.
    c. nitrates.
    d. phytochemicals.

25. All of the following are true regarding regular consumption of hot dogs, luncheon meats, and vegetables preserved with nitrates EXCEPT:
    a. it increases the risk of cancer of the liver.
    b. it increases the risk of cancer of the stomach.
    c. bacon and pickled vegetables contain high levels.
    d. most cancer cases associated with nitrates occur in the U.S.

26. Excessive consumption of alcohol has been linked to development of all of the following types of cancer EXCEPT:
    a. stomach.
    b. breast.
    c. mouth.
    d. throat.

27. Obesity characterized by fat stores in the _____ region of the body increases the risk for cancer development.
    a. shoulders
    b. central
    c. lower
    d. hip

28. All of the following are considered bogus treatments or prevention strategies for cancer EXCEPT:
    a. macrobiotic diets.
    b. hydrogen peroxide.
    c. laetrile tablets.
    d. high intake of fruits and vegetables.

29. Cancer-preventing habits include all of the following EXCEPT:
    a. not smoking.
    b. consuming 5+ servings of vegetables and fruits per day.
    c. physical inactivity.
    d. a low-saturated fat diet.

30. All of the following are phytochemicals that have antioxidant abilities EXCEPT:
    a. lycopene.
    b. lutein.
    c. flavonoids.
    d. nitrates.

To check yourself, use the answer key at the bottom of the page.[23]

---

[23] 1. c, 2. d, 3. a, 4. c, 5. b, 6. d, 7. b, 8. d, 9. c, 10. b, 11. a, 12. b, 13. d, 14. c, 15. a, 16. d, 17. b, 18. c, 19. a, 20. d, 21. c, 22. c, 23. b, 24. c, 25. d, 26. a, 27. b, 28. d, 29. c, 30. d

Unit 23 – Good Things to Know about Minerals

Key Concepts

- Minerals are single atoms that cannot be created or destroyed by the human body or by any other ordinary means.
- Minerals serve as components of body structures and play key roles in the regulation of body processes.
- Deficiency diseases occur when too little of any of the 15 essential minerals are provided to the body, and overdose reactions occur when too much is provided.
- Inadequate intakes of certain minerals are associated with the development of chronic disorders, including osteoporosis, iron deficiency, and hypertension.

Unit Outline

I. Mineral facts
   A. Getting a charge out of minerals
      1. Charge problems
      2. Preserving the mineral content of food
      3. The boundaries of this unit
II. Selected minerals: Calcium
   A. A short primer on bones
      1. Teeth are a type of bone
      2. Remodeling your bones
   B. Osteoporosis
      1. The timing of bone formation
      2. How do you build and maintain dense bones?
         a. The current D controversy
      3. We are consuming too little calcium
         a. Why do women consume too little calcium?
      4. What else influences osteoporosis?
      5. How is osteoporosis treated?
   C. Calcium: Where to find it
      1. Watch for calcium on the label
      2. Can you consume too much calcium?
III. Selected minerals: Iron
   A. The role of iron in hemoglobin and myoglobin
   B. Iron deficiency is a big problem
      1. Consequences of iron deficiency
   C. Getting enough iron in your diet
      1. Overdosing on iron
IV. Selected minerals: Sodium
   A. What does sodium do in the body?
      1. A bit about blood pressure
      2. What causes hypertension?
      3. Salt sensitivity
      4. Other risk factors for hypertension
      5. How is hypertension treated?
      6. Cutting back on salt
      7. Label watch

Unit Glossary

- **minerals:** In the context of nutrition, minerals are specific, single atoms that perform particular functions in the body. There are 15 essential minerals—or minerals required in the diet.
- **cofactors:** Individual minerals required for the activity of certain proteins.
- **remodeling:** The breakdown and buildup of bone tissue.
- **osteoporosis** (osteo = bones; poro = porous, osis = abnormal condition): A condition characterized by porous bones; it is due to the loss of minerals from the bones.
- **hemoglobin:** The iron-containing protein in red blood cells.
- **myoglobin:** The iron-containing protein in muscle cells.
- **iron deficiency:** A disorder that results from a depletion of iron stores in the body. It is characterized by weakness, fatigue, short attention span, poor appetite, increased susceptibility to infection, and irritability.
- **iron-deficiency anemia:** A condition that results when the content of hemoglobin in red blood cells is reduced due to a lack of iron. It is characterized by the signs of iron deficiency plus paleness, exhaustion, and a rapid heart rate.
- **water balance:** The ratio of the amount of water outside cells to the amount inside cells; a proper balance is needed for normal cell functioning.
- **hypertension:** High blood pressure. It is defined as blood pressure exerted inside blood vessel walls that typically exceeds 140/90 millimeters of mercury.
- **essential hypertension:** Hypertension of no known cause; also called primary or idiopathic hypertension, it accounts for 95% of all cases of hypertension.
- **salt sensitivity:** A genetically influenced condition in which a person's blood pressure rises when high amounts of salt or sodium are consumed. Such individuals are sometimes identified by blood pressure increases of 10% or more when switched from a low-salt to a high-salt diet.

Practice Multiple-Choice Test

1. Specific single atoms that perform specific functions in the body are called:
   a. vitamins.
   b. minerals.
   c. phytochemicals.
   d. water.

2. All of the following are true regarding minerals EXCEPT:
   a. the body contains 40 or more.
   b. 15 are considered essential.
   c. they consist of 2 or more atoms.
   d. they carry a positive or negative charge.

3. What is the name of a condition characterized by porous bones due to the loss of minerals from the bones?
   a. Rickets
   b. Osteoporosis
   c. Bone cancer
   d. Bow leg syndrome

122

4. Iron-deficiency anemia is characterized by all of the following EXCEPT:
   a. the content of hemoglobin in red blood cells is reduced.
   b. it shares the same characteristics as iron deficiency.
   c. symptoms include rapid heart rate.
   d. symptoms include flushed appearance.

5. All of the following are true regarding iodine EXCEPT:
   a. deficiency results in goiter.
   b. deficiency results in cretinism.
   c. it acts as an antioxidant.
   d. most of the iodine in our diet comes from iodized salt.

6. Which of the following minerals is a component of teeth enamel?
   a. Iodine
   b. Fluoride
   c. Copper
   d. Selenium

7. All of the following are risk factors for osteoporosis EXCEPT:
   a. menopause.
   b. Caucasian or Asian heritage.
   c. overweight.
   d. cigarette smoking.

8. The iron-containing protein in red blood cells is called:
   a. myoglobin.
   b. hemoglobin.
   c. a cofactor.
   d. a coenzyme.

9. All of the following are true of hypertension EXCEPT:
   a. it is another term for high blood pressure.
   b. it is defined as blood pressure >140/90.
   c. it is a major health problem in the U.S.
   d. it is considered a disease in its own right.

10. The DASH diet consists of a daily eating pattern made up of all of the following food groups EXCEPT:
   a. 2-3 servings of vegetables.
   b. 4-5 servings of fruits.
   c. 7-8 servings of grains.
   d. 2-3 servings of low-fat dairy products.

11. Minerals provide:
   a. 4 calories per gram.
   b. 7 calories per gram.
   c. 9 calories per gram.
   d. no calories.

12. Individual minerals that are required for the activity of certain proteins are called:
    a. coenzymes.
    b. cofactors.
    c. collaborators.
    d. coordinators.

13. All of the following are examples of a mineral serving as a cofactor EXCEPT:
    a. iron is needed for hemoglobin's function in oxygen and carbon dioxide transport.
    b. zinc is needed to activate or is a component of over 200 enzymes.
    c. magnesium activates over 300 enzymes involved in the formation of energy and proteins.
    d. beta-carotene serves as a precursor to the formation of vitamin A.

14. Remodeling refers to:
    a. the breakdown and buildup of bone tissue.
    b. the permanent destruction of bone tissue.
    c. the excessive buildup of bone tissue.
    d. loss of minerals from the bone.

15. All of the following are true regarding phosphorus EXCEPT:
    a. it transports oxygen as a component of hemoglobin.
    b. it is a component of bones and teeth.
    c. it is necessary to maintain the right acid-base balance of body fluids.
    d. milk products are a good food source.

16. All of the following are true regarding calcium EXCEPT:
    a. it is a component of bones and teeth.
    b. it is needed for muscle and nerve activity.
    c. deficiency results in osteoporosis in adults.
    d. the average intake of calcium among U.S. women is approximately 75% of the DRI.

17. All of the following are true regarding magnesium EXCEPT:
    a. deficiency results in stunted growth in children.
    b. it is needed for nerve activity.
    c. overdose results in hemochromatosis.
    d. plant foods are a good source.

18. All of the following are true regarding iron EXCEPT:
    a. it transports oxygen as a component of hemoglobin in red blood cells.
    b. cooking foods in iron pans increases the iron content of foods.
    c. overdose can result in atherosclerosis in adults.
    d. milk products are a good food source.

19. All of the following are true regarding zinc EXCEPT:
    a. plant foods are a good source.
    b. deficiency results in growth failure.
    c. it is a component of insulin and many enzymes.
    d. supplements may decrease the duration and severity of the common cold.

124

20. Which of the following minerals acts as an antioxidant in conjunction with vitamin E?
    a. Magnesium
    b. Selenium
    c. Zinc
    d. Calcium

21. The mineral that is required for the normal utilization of glucose and fat is called:
    a. molybdenum.
    b. manganese.
    c. iron.
    d. chromium.

22. All of the following are true regarding copper EXCEPT:
    a. it is a component of thyroid hormones.
    b. it functions in immunity, growth, and glucose utilization.
    c. overdose results in Wilson's disease.
    d. a good food source is seafood.

23. All of the following are true regarding sodium EXCEPT:
    a. it is needed to maintain the right acid-base balance in body fluids.
    b. the AI for men and women is 2300 milligrams.
    c. deficiency results in muscle cramps.
    d. processed foods are the leading source of dietary sodium.

24. Which of the following are most important for increasing bone mass before the age of 30?
    a. Adequate calcium and vitamin C intake
    b. Adequate calcium and vitamin E intake
    c. Adequate calcium and magnesium intake
    d. Adequate calcium and vitamin D intake

25. All of the following behaviors help to prevent osteoporosis EXCEPT:
    a. getting regular physical activity.
    b. consuming recommended intakes of calcium (500 mg for children, 800 mg for adults).
    c. not smoking.
    d. moderate alcohol intake.

26. Approaches to the treatment of osteoporosis include all of the following EXCEPT:
    a. regular weight-bearing exercise.
    b. 3-4 servings of fruits and vegetables daily.
    c. adequate calcium and vitamin D intake.
    d. medication.

27. All of the following are true regarding iron deficiency EXCEPT:
    a. it results from depletion of iron stores in the body.
    b. it results in weakness.
    c. it results in increased appetite.
    d. it results in increased susceptibility to infection.

28. A genetically influenced condition in which a person's blood pressure rises when high amounts of sodium are consumed is called:
    a. essential hypertension.
    b. hypertension.
    c. salt sensitivity.
    d. prehypertension.

29. All of the following are risk factors for hypertension EXCEPT:
    a. family history.
    b. high vegetable and fruit intake.
    c. obesity.
    d. physical inactivity.

30. All of the following are approaches to treat hypertension EXCEPT:
    a. the DASH diet.
    b. weight loss if needed.
    c. intake of less than 4000 mg of sodium per day.
    d. regular physical activity.

To check yourself, use the answer key at the bottom of the page.[24]

_____

[24] 1. b, 2. c, 3. b, 4. d, 5. c, 6. b, 7. c, 8. b, 9. d, 10. a, 11. d, 12. b, 13. d, 14. a, 15. a, 16. d, 17. c, 18. d, 19. a, 20. b, 21. d, 22. a, 23. b, 24. d, 25. b, 26. b, 27. c, 28. c, 29. b, 30. c

Unit 24 – Dietary Supplements and Functional Foods

Key Concepts

- Dietary supplements include vitamin and mineral pills, herbal remedies, proteins and amino acids, fish oils, and other products.
- Dietary supplements do not have to be shown to be safe or effective prior to being sold.
- Although food is the preferred source of vitamins and minerals, certain people benefit from judiciously selected vitamin or mineral supplements.
- Prebiotics and probiotics can benefit health.

Unit Outline

I. Dietary supplements
   A. Regulation of dietary supplements
   B. Vitamin and mineral supplements
      1. Vitamin and mineral supplements: Who benefits?
         a. Using vitamin and mineral supplements for the wrong reason
         b. The rational use of vitamin and mineral supplements
   C. Herbal remedies
      1. Effects of herbal remedies
         a. Which herbal supplements are potentially beneficial?
         b. Ephedra (ma huang)
      2. A measure of quality assurance for dietary supplements
II. Functional foods
   A. Prebiotics and probiotics: From "pharm" to table
   B. Final thoughts

Unit Glossary

- **dietary supplements:** Any products intended to supplement the diet, including vitamin and mineral supplements; proteins, enzymes, and amino acids; fish oils and fatty acids; hormones and hormone precursors; and herbs and other plant extracts. Such products must be labeled "Dietary Supplement."
- **bioavailability:** The amount of a nutrient consumed that is available for absorption and use by the body.
- **functional foods:** Generally taken to mean foods, fortified foods, and enhanced food products that may benefit health beyond the effects of essential nutrients they contain.
- **prebiotics:** Non-digestible food ingredients that beneficially affect a person by selectively stimulating the growth or activity of one or a limited number of bacteria in the colon. Inulin, an extract from chicory root, is a common prebiotic. Also called "intestinal fertilizer."
- **probiotics:** Live microorganisms which, when delivered in adequate amounts, confer a health benefit. Strains of *Lactobacillus* (lac-toebah-sil-us) and *Bifidobacteria* (bif-id-dough bacteria) are the best-known probiotics. Also called "friendly bacteria."

Practice Multiple-Choice Test

1. A dietary supplement might include all of the following EXCEPT:
   a. vitamins and minerals.
   b. herbs (botanicals).
   c. aspirin.
   d. proteins and amino acids.

2. All of the following are FDA regulations regarding dietary supplement labeling EXCEPT:
   a. the product must have a "Nutrition Facts" panel.
   b. the product must be labeled "dietary supplement."
   c. the product must have a "Supplement Facts" panel.
   d. qualifying nutrient claims can be placed on labels.

3. All of the following groups may benefit from vitamin and mineral supplements EXCEPT:
   a. vegans.
   b. people with alcoholism.
   c. people living in areas with a fluoridated water supply.
   d. newborns.

4. Which two herbs have a laxative effect?
   a. Cranberry and rose hips
   b. Cranberry and senna
   c. Senna and rose hips
   d. Rose hips and ginger

5. All of the following are private groups that test herbal supplements for disintegration, purity, potency, and labeling EXCEPT:
   a. U.S. Pharmacopeia (USP).
   b. Consumer Laboratories (CL).
   c. the Food and Drug Administration (FDA).
   d. National Formulary (NF).

6. Foods are made "functional" by all of the following methods EXCEPT:
   a. taking out potentially harmful components.
   b. genetically modifying them.
   c. increasing the amount of nutrients and beneficial nonnutrients.
   d. using beneficial substances in food production.

7. A functional food that has been shown to reduce blood levels of LDL cholesterol is:
   a. grape juice.
   b. green tea.
   c. probiotics.
   d. stanol- and sterol-fortified margarine.

8. Food sources of prebiotics include all of the following EXCEPT:
   a. chicory.
   b. fermented products.
   c. wheat.
   d. barley.

9. Strains of *Lactobacillus* and *Bifidobacteria* that have beneficial effects on the body are called:
   a. probiotics.
   b. antibiotics.
   c. prebiotics.
   d. postbiotics.

10. Any product intended to supplement the diet, including vitamins, minerals, enzymes, and others, must be labeled:
   a. "botanical."
   b. "neutraceutical."
   c. "herbal remedy."
   d. "dietary supplement."

11. The name of the governmental act passed by Congress in 1994 that minimally regulates dietary supplements is called:
   a. the Nutrition Facts Labeling Act.
   b. the Dietary Supplement Health and Education Act.
   c. the Consumer Protection and Dietary Supplement Act.
   d. the Food Safety Protection Act.

12. The Supplement Facts label must contain all of the following information EXCEPT:
   a. serving size.
   b. ingredients.
   c. total calories.
   d. percent Daily Values.

13. The governmental body responsible for regulating claims for dietary supplements in advertisements is the:
   a. USDA.
   b. EPA.
   c. FDA.
   d. FTC.

14. The Federal Trade Commission regulates claims made for dietary supplements in all of the following EXCEPT:
   a. newspaper articles.
   b. broadcast advertisements.
   c. Internet site advertisements.
   d. infomercials.

15. The amount of a nutrient consumed that is available for absorption and use by the body is called:
   a. biofeedback.
   b. bivalent.
   c. bioavailability.
   d. biological value.

16. Dietary supplements are NOT considered an effective remedy for any of the following EXCEPT:
   a. chronic fatigue syndrome.
   b. adults with rheumatoid arthritis.
   c. hair loss.
   d. stress.

17. All of the following are guidelines for choosing and using vitamin and mineral supplements EXCEPT:
    a. "Purchase supplements labeled 'USP.'"
    b. "Take supplements with meals."
    c. "Consult your healthcare provider before you take supplements to treat a problem."
    d. "Choose supplements containing 150% of the Daily Value or less."

18. All of the following are true regarding herbal remedies EXCEPT:
    a. approximately 30% of all modern drugs are derived from plants.
    b. approximately 75% of U.S. adults use herbal supplements each year.
    c. plant products known to treat disease are considered drugs.
    d. plants that have not demonstrated safety are considered herbs.

19. All of the following herbal remedies have been shown to be beneficial EXCEPT:
    a. ephedra.
    b. gingko biloba.
    c. cranberry.
    d. SAMe.

20. Dietary supplements that are likely ineffective or unsafe include all of the following EXCEPT:
    a. apricot pits.
    b. skullcap.
    c. DHEA.
    d. kava.

21. All of the following are true regarding ginseng EXCEPT:
    a. one of its proposed uses is to increase energy.
    b. one of its proposed uses is to relieve mild depression.
    c. a potential side effect is insomnia.
    d. one of its proposed uses is to stimulate immune function.

22. The herb that may decrease symptoms in patients with Alzheimer's disease and increase blood flow to the brain is called:
    a. garlic.
    b. Saint John's wort.
    c. DHEA.
    d. gingko biloba.

23. Which of the following herbs may prevent motion sickness?:
    a. Cranberry
    b. Senna
    c. Ginger
    d. Garlic

24. All of the following have been used in the treatment of mild depression EXCEPT:
    a. rose hips.
    b. Saint John's wort.
    c. SAMe.
    d. DHEA.

130

25. All of the following are considerations for the use of herbal supplements EXCEPT:
    a. investigate safety by talking to the staff at health food stores.
    b. do not use herbs if pregnant or breastfeeding.
    c. if you take prescriptions, clear the use of herbal remedies with your doctor.
    d. buy herbs labeled with "USP," "CL," or "NF."

26. Foods, fortified foods, and enhanced food products that may benefit health beyond the effects of essential nutrients they contain are called:
    a. enriched foods.
    b. supplemental foods.
    c. enhanced foods.
    d. functional foods.

27. Certain fiber-like forms of nondigestible carbohydrates that support the growth of beneficial bacteria in the gut are called:
    a. probiotics.
    b. antibiotics.
    c. prebiotics.
    d. postbiotics.

28. Food sources of probiotics include all of the following EXCEPT:
    a. yogurt with live cultures.
    b. kefir.
    c. onions.
    d. breast milk.

29. All of the following are potential benefits of prebiotics and probiotics EXCEPT:
    a. prevention of diarrhea and constipation.
    b. decreased risk of obesity.
    c. treatment of lactose intolerance.
    d. decreased blood cholesterol levels.

30. All of the following functional foods may decrease the risk of certain cancers EXCEPT:
    a. cranberry juice.
    b. green tea.
    c. cruciferous vegetables.
    d. tomato products.

To check yourself, use the answer key at the bottom of the page.[25]

---

[25] 1. c, 2. a, 3. c, 4. c, 5. c, 6. b, 7. d, 8. b, 9. a, 10. d, 11. b, 12. c, 13. d, 14. a, 15. c, 16. b, 17. d, 18. b, 19. a, 20. c, 21. b, 22. d, 23. c, 24. a, 25. a, 26. d, 27. c, 28. c, 29. b, 30. a

Unit 25 – Water Is an Essential Nutrient

Key Concepts

- Water is an essential nutrient. It is a required part of the diet. Deficiency symptoms develop when too little is consumed, and toxicity symptoms occur when too much is ingested.
- Functions of water include maintenance of body hydration and temperature, facilitation of digestion, removal of waste products, and participation in energy formation. It is our major source of fluoride.
- Water is a precious resource whose availability and quality are threatened by wasteful use and pollution.

Unit Outline

I. Water: Where would we be without it?
   A. Water's roles as an essential nutrient
      1. Water, water, everywhere
         a. Most foods contain lots of water, too
      2. Health benefits of water
   B. The nature of our water supply
      1. Does the earth supply "gourmet" water?
         a. Is bottled water safe?
         b. Water gimmicks
      2. Fluoridated bottled water
   C. Meeting our need for water
      1. Are caffeine-containing beverages hydrating?
   D. Water deficiency
   E. Water toxicity

Practice Multiple-Choice Test

1. All of the following are important points about water EXCEPT:
   a. our need is measured in cups not grams or milligrams.
   b. without it life expectancy is about 2 weeks.
   c. it is the largest single component of our diet.
   d. it is the largest single component of our body.

2. Key functions of water in the body include all of the following EXCEPT:
   a. it provides energy.
   b. it provides a medium for chemical reactions.
   c. it transports nutrients and waste products.
   d. it helps regulate body temperature.

3. Adults are approximately what percentage of water by weight?
   a. 20 to 25%
   b. 60 to 65%
   c. 30 to 35%
   d. 80 to 85%

4. Which of the following foods has the highest content of water?
   a. Tomato
   b. Egg
   c. Bread
   d. Oil

5. All of the following are true regarding fresh drinking water around the world EXCEPT:
   a. population growth worldwide is increasing the demand for water.
   b. about half of the world's water supply is fresh water.
   c. water is highly prized in the Middle East.
   d. water scarcity is a primary concern in many nations.

6. All of the following factors are contributing to dwindling water supplies EXCEPT:
   a. increased awareness.
   b. groundwater depletion.
   c. pollution.
   d. wasteful use of water.

7. All of the following are advantages of bottled waters EXCEPT:
   a. they are calorie free.
   b. they are generally low in sodium or sodium free.
   c. they are a healthier choice than soft drinks.
   d. they are more "pure" and therefore better for you.

8. All of the following describe bottled water and fluoridation EXCEPT:
   a. some bottled waters do not contain fluoride.
   b. fluoride is listed on the label if added.
   c. fluoride is important to prevent tooth decay.
   d. the bottled water industry has been praised for the lack of fluoride.

9. All of the following increase a person's need for water EXCEPT:
   a. physical activity.
   b. exposure to cold weather.
   c. exposure to high altitudes.
   d. high intake of fruits and vegetables.

10. All of the following are true regarding water toxicity EXCEPT:
    a. it is called hyponatremia.
    b. it has occurred in infants given overdiluted infant formula.
    c. it has occurred in marathon runners.
    d. it is not life threatening.

11. Water qualifies as an essential nutrient for all of the following reasons EXCEPT:
    a. it performs specific functions in the body.
    b. deficiency symptoms develop when too little is consumed.
    c. it is not a required part of our diet.
    d. toxicity symptoms develop when too much is consumed.

12. The roles that water plays in energy formation include all of the following EXCEPT:
    a. it is produced as an end product of energy formation from carbohydrates.
    b. it is produced as an end product of energy formation from proteins.
    c. it is produced as an end product of energy formation from fats.
    d. production and excretion of water and energy production stop when intake stops.

13. Which of the following is true regarding water intake?
    a. It cures chronic fatigue.
    b. It flushes out toxins.
    c. It regulates body temperature.
    d. It prevents dry, wrinkled skin.

14. Which of the following foods does NOT contain water?
    a. Cooked hamburger
    b. Butter
    c. Oil
    d. Swiss cheese

15. The proportion of water in body tissues is approximately:
    a. 90% in blood, 50% in muscle, 10% in bone, and 25% in fat.
    b. 75% in blood, 50% in muscle, 10% in bone, and 80% in fat.
    c. 83% in blood, 50% in muscle, 22% in bone, and 10% in fat.
    d. 83% in blood, 75% in muscle, 22% in bone, and 10% in fat.

16. On average, what percentage of our water intake comes from the foods that we eat?
    a. 11%
    b. 25%
    c. 4%
    d. 19%

17. All of the following are true regarding water EXCEPT:
    a. fruits and vegetables contain approximately 75% to 90% water.
    b. it is easily possible to meet our water needs through solid foods alone.
    c. meats contain between 50 and 70% water.
    d. most beverages are more than 85% water.

18. Consumption of over _____ of fluid each day is associated with a decreased risk of bladder, breast, and colon cancer.
    a. 10 cups
    b. 8 cups
    c. 6 cups
    d. 4 cups

19. All of the following are true regarding the Earth's water supply EXCEPT:
    a. 97% is salt water.
    b. 3% is fresh water.
    c. not all fresh water is considered drinkable.
    d. water scarcity is not a concern in most countries.

134

20. The agency responsible for the safety of public water supplies in the U.S. is the:
    a. FDA.
    b. USDA.
    c. EPA.
    d. FTC.

21. Which of the following describes mineral water?
    a. Taken from protected underground reservoirs lodged between layers of rock
    b. Taken from freshwater springs that form pools or streams on the earth's surface
    c. Naturally carbonated water
    d. Tap water

22. Which of the following describes spring water?
    a. Taken from protected underground reservoirs lodged between layers of rock
    b. Taken from freshwater springs that form pools or streams on the earth's surface
    c. Naturally carbonated water
    d. Tap water

23. Which of the following describes "true" sparkling water?
    a. Taken from protected underground reservoirs lodged between layers of rock
    b. Taken from freshwater springs that form pools or streams on the earth's surface
    c. Naturally carbonated water
    d. Tap water

24. Approximately what percentage of bottled waters sold in the U.S. contain tap water?
    a. 25%
    b. 5%
    c. 15%
    c. None

25. Which federal agency regulates bottled water?
    a. USDA
    b. FDA
    c. EPA
    d. FTC

26. The Adequate Intake (AI) of water from fluids and foods for women is:
    a. 15 cups.
    b. 12 cups.
    c. 11 cups.
    d. 8 cups.

27. The Adequate Intake (AI) of water from fluids and foods for men is:
    a. 15 cups.
    b. 12 cups.
    c. 11 cups.
    d. 8 cups.

28. All of the following increase a person's need for water EXCEPT:
    a. high-protein diets.
    b. high-fiber diets.
    c. alcohol intake.
    d. coffee intake.

29. All of the following are true regarding dehydration EXCEPT:
    a. it results from water deficiency.
    b. it is not life threatening.
    c. it can result in kidney failure.
    d. symptoms include dizziness and nausea.

30. A good way to check if you are adequately hydrated is to check the color of your urine which should:
    a. be bright yellow.
    b. have a green tinge.
    c. be pale yellow.
    d. be orange.

To check yourself, use the answer key at the bottom of the page.[26]

_____

[26] 1. b, 2. a, 3. b, 4. a, 5. b, 6. a, 7. d, 8. d, 9. d, 10. d, 11. c, 12. d, 13. c, 14. c, 15. d, 16. d, 17. b, 18. a, 19. d, 20. c, 21. a, 22. b, 23. c, 24. a, 25. b, 26. c, 27. a, 28. d, 29. b, 30. c

Unit 26 – Nutrient-Gene Interactions in Health and Disease

Key Concepts

- Nutrients interact in important ways with gene functions and thereby affect health status. Nutrients can turn genes on or off, and nutrient intake can compensate for abnormally functioning genes.
- Health problems related to nutrient–gene interactions originate within cells.
- Advances in knowledge of nutrient–gene interactions are dramatically changing nutritional approaches to disease prevention and treatment.

Unit Outline

I. Nutrition and genomics
   A. Diet-gene interactions
   B. Genetic secrets unfolded
   C. Single-gene defects
II. Chronic disease: Nurture and nature
   A. Cancer
   B. Hypertension
   C. Obesity
   D. Genetics of food selection
III. Nutrition Tomorrow
IV. Are gene-based designer diets in your future?

Unit Glossary

- **genome:** Combined term for "genes" and "chromosomes." It represents all the genes and DNA contained in an organism, which are principally located in chromosomes. The human genome consists of 20,000 to 24,000 genes.
- **genes:** The basic units of heredity that occupy specific places (loci) on chromosomes. Genes consist of large DNA molecules, each of which contains the code for the manufacture of a specific enzyme or other protein.
- **genotype:** The specific genetic makeup of an individual as coded by DNA.
- **genomics:** The study of the functions and interactions of all genes in the genome. Unlike genetics, it includes the study of genes related to common conditions and their interaction with environmental factors.
- **nutrigenomics:** The study of nutrient-related functions and interactions with genes and their affects on health and disease.
- **chromosomes:** Structures in the nuclei of cells that contain genes. Humans have 23 pairs of chromosomes; half of each pair comes from the mother and half from the father.
- **DNA (deoxyribonucleic acid):** Segments of genes that provide instructions for the manufacture of enzymes and other proteins by cells. DNA looks something like an immensely long ladder twisted into a helix, or coil. The sides of the ladder structure of DNA are formed by a backbone of sugar-phosphate molecules, and the "rungs" consist of pairs of bases joined by weak chemical bonds. Bases are the "letters" that spell out the genetic code, and there are over 3 billion of them in human DNA. There are two types of base pairs: adenine-guanine and cytosinethymine. Each sequence of three base pairs on DNA codes for a specific amino acid. A specific enzyme or other protein is formed when coded amino acids are collected and strung together in the sequence dictated by DNA. Some sections of DNA do not transmit genetic information because they don't code for protein production. They appear to signal which genes will turn on and how long they will be activated. Characteristics of these segments of DNA vary among individuals, making it possible to identify individuals based on "DNA fingerprinting."

- **DNA fingerprinting:** The process of identifying specific individuals by their DNA. This is possible because no two individuals have the same genetic makeup. Differences among individuals are due to variations in the sections of DNA molecules that do not transmit genetic information.
- **single-gene defects:** Disorders resulting from one abnormal gene. Also called "inborn errors of metabolism." Over 6,000 single-gene defects have been cataloged, and most are very rare.
- **salt sensitivity:** A genetically determined condition in which a person's blood pressure rises when high amounts of salt or sodium are consumed. Such individuals are sometimes identified by blood pressure increases of 10% or more when switched from a lower-salt (1 to 3 grams) to a higher-salt (12 to 15 grams) diet.

Practice Multiple-Choice Test

1. All of the following are examples of the effects gene types have on the body's response to nutritional factors EXCEPT:
    a. whole oats lowering blood cholesterol.
    b. high folate intake decreasing the risk of cancer.
    c. high alcohol intake during pregnancy producing physical abnormalities in the fetus.
    d. low-carbohydrate diets increasing the risk of type 2 diabetes.

2. Segments of genes that provide instructions for the manufacture of enzymes and other proteins by cells are called:
    a. genes.
    b. RNA.
    c. DNA.
    d. chromosomes.

3. The combined term for "genes" and "chromosomes" is:
    a. nutrigenomics.
    b. genotype.
    c. genome.
    d. genominotics.

4. The structure of DNA is referred to as a:
    a. ladder.
    b. helix.
    c. spiral.
    d. wave.

5. The amount of plaque that builds up in arteries is influenced by which of the following? (Choose the best answer.)
    a. Single environmental factor
    b. Single genetic factor
    c. Multiple environmental factors
    d. Multiple environmental and genetic factors

6. Which of the following types of cancer is related to environmental factors, not genetic factors?
    a. Prostate
    b. Pancreas
    c. Endometrial
    d. Colon

138

7. Obesity is an interaction of all of the following EXCEPT:
    a. sensitivity to salt.
    b. nutritional factors.
    c. environmental factors.
    d. genetic factors.

8. Which of the following statements is true?
    a. Lacking the gene that codes for an enzyme that helps the body excrete a specific sulfur-containing chemical unique to cruciferous vegetables is a risk factor for cancer.
    b. Nutrients do not affect the expression of genes.
    c. All individuals who consume a high-saturated fat diet develop hardened arteries.
    d. Most cancers are related primarily to environmental factors.

9. The study of diet- and nutrient-related functions and interactions of genes and their affects on health and disease is called:
    a. genomics.
    b. nutrigenomics.
    c. DNA fingerprinting.
    d. DNA blueprinting.

10. All of the following are true regarding cancer EXCEPT:
    a. high-fat diets increase risk.
    b. some cancers have genetic components that interact with environmental factors.
    c. high levels of body fat increase risk.
    d. alcohol intake lowers risk.

11. The basic units of heredity that occupy specific places on chromosomes are called:
    a. genomes.
    b. chromosomes.
    c. DNA.
    d. genes.

12. The specific genetic makeup of an individual as coded by DNA is called:
    a. DNA fingerprinting.
    b. genotype.
    c. genes.
    d. chromosomes.

13. The study of the functions and interactions of all genes in the genome including the study of genes related to common conditions is called:
    a. genomics.
    b. nutrigenomics.
    c. DNA fingerprinting.
    d. DNA blueprinting.

14. The process of identifying specific individuals by their DNA is called:
    a. DNA fingerprinting.
    b. DNA blueprinting.
    c. DNA coding.
    d. DNA analysis.

15. Genomics is unlike genetics because it includes the study of genes related to:
    a. common conditions and their interaction with single traits.
    b. common conditions and their interaction with single genes.
    c. common conditions and their interaction with environmental factors.
    d. common conditions and their interaction with physical activity.

16. Disorders resulting from one abnormal gene are called:
    a. hereditary disorders.
    b. single-gene disorders.
    c. genetic malfunction.
    d. gene disruption.

17. All of the following are true regarding the genes in our bodies EXCEPT:
    a. our genes have been around for 4000 years.
    b. genes replicate themselves exactly over generations.
    c. lasting modifications in genes almost never occur.
    d. changes in genetic traits do not account for increases in the incidence of a disease.

18. Which of the following is true regarding changes in genetic traits?
    a. Changes in genetic traits are most likely the cause for the increase in the rates of obesity.
    b. Changes in genetic traits are most likely the cause for the decrease in the rates of heart disease.
    c. Lasting modifications in genes almost never occur.
    d. Changes in genetic traits are most likely the cause for the increase in the rates of diabetes.

19. How alike are humans genetically?
    a. 0.1%
    b. 10%
    c. 50%
    d. 99.9%

20. What percent of our genes is responsible for making each individual distinct?
    a. 0.1%
    b. 10%
    c. 50%
    d. 99.9%

21. A very rare disorder that is caused by the lack of an enzyme and that causes the build-up of phenylalanine in the blood is called:
    a. celiac disease.
    b. lactose intolerance.
    c. PKU.
    d. hemochromatosis.

22. High levels of phenylalanine in the blood during growth leads to which of the following?
    a. Mental retardation
    b. Intestinal malabsorption
    c. Plaque build-up in the arteries
    d. Cancer

140

23. An intestinal malabsorption disorder caused by an inherited intolerance to gluten in wheat, rye, and barley is called:
    a. celiac disease.
    b. lactose intolerance.
    c. PKU.
    d. hemochromatosis.

24. A disorder resulting from lack of the enzyme lactase is called:
    a. celiac disease.
    b. lactose intolerance.
    c. PKU.
    d. hemochromatosis.

25. A disorder due to a genetic deficiency of a protein that helps to regulate iron absorption is called:
    a. celiac disease.
    b. lactose intolerance.
    c. PKU.
    d. hemochromatosis.

26. All of the following are examples of single-gene disorders that affect nutritional needs EXCEPT:
    a. endometrial cancer.
    b. phenylketonuria.
    c. lactose intolerance.
    d. hemochromatosis.

27. All of the following describe salt sensitivity EXCEPT:
    a. it is a genetically determined condition.
    b. high intakes of sodium increase the blood pressure of people with this condition.
    c. approximately 51% of people with hypertension are salt sensitive.
    d. approximately 10% of people with normal blood pressure are salt sensitive.

28. All of the following factors contribute to the development of hypertension EXCEPT:
    a. high body fat.
    b. regular physical activity.
    c. genetic traits.
    d. high alcohol intake.

29. All of the following are true regarding obesity EXCEPT:
    a. over 200 genetic traits have been associated with obesity development.
    b. it is primarily influenced by a low-calorie diet.
    c. high-carbohydrate diets may influence obesity development in some people.
    d. a genetic predisposition toward inactivity may influence obesity development in some people.

30. All of the following are true regarding food preferences EXCEPT:
    a. they are largely learned.
    b. there are over 80 genes that help people taste bitter foods.
    c. people with a high sensitivity to bitter tastes tend to like cabbage and Brussels sprouts.
    d. a genetic tendency to avoid bitter vegetables may be linked to disease development.

To check yourself, use the answer key at the bottom of the page.[27]

---

[27] 1. d, 2. c, 3. c, 4. b, 5. d, 6. c, 7. a, 8. d, 9. b, 10. d, 11. d, 12. b, 13. a, 14. a, 15. c, 16. b, 17. a, 18. c, 19. d, 20. a, 21. c, 22. a, 23. a, 24. b, 25. d, 26. a, 27. d, 28. b, 29. b, 30. c

Unit 27 – Nutrition and Physical Fitness for Everyone

Key Concepts

- Physical fitness, along with a good diet, confers a number of physical and mental health benefits.
- You don't have to be an athlete or be lean to be physically fit. Fitness depends primarily on muscular strength, endurance, and flexibility.
- People who are physically fit have respiratory and circulatory systems capable of delivering large amounts of oxygen to muscles and muscular systems that can utilize large amounts of oxygen for prolonged periods of time.
- Physical fitness can be achieved by resistance training, aerobic exercises, and stretching.
- The fitness level of most people in the United States is poor.

Unit Outline

I. Physical fitness: It offers something for everyone
   A. The "happy consequences" of physical activity
      1. The bonus pack: Exercise plus a good diet
         a. Exercise and body weight
   B. Physical activity and fitness
      1. Muscle strength
      2. Endurance: A measure of aerobic fitness
         a. How is aerobic fitness determined?
         b. How do you know your VO_2 max?
         c. How do you know your heart rate?
II. Nutrition and fitness
   A. Muscle fuel
      1. Stiff muscles in the out of shape
   B. Diet and aerobic fitness
   C. A reminder about water
III. A personal fitness program
   A. Becoming physically fit: What it takes
      1. A resistance training plan
   B. The aerobic fitness plan
      1. Some exercise is much better than none
      2. The caloric value of exercise
   C. Population-based physical activity recommendations
      1. A cautionary note
         a. The paradox of death during exercise
IV. U.S. fitness: America needs to shape up
   A. A focus on fitness in children

Unit Glossary

- **physical fitness**: The health of the body as measured by muscular strength, endurance, and flexibility in the conduct of physical activity.
- **aerobic fitness:** A state of respiratory and circulatory health as measured by the ability to deliver oxygen to muscles and the capacity of muscles to use the oxygen for physical activity.
- **maximal oxygen consumption:** The highest amount of oxygen that can be delivered to, and used by, muscles for physical activity. Also called VO_2 max and maximal volume of oxygen.

Practice Multiple-Choice Test

1. All of the following are benefits of regular physical activity EXCEPT:
    a. reduced risk of heart disease.
    b. increased abdominal fat.
    c. decreased risk of hypertension.
    d. decreased risk of osteoporosis.

2. All of the following are true regarding maximal oxygen consumption EXCEPT:
    a. it is abbreviated VO_2 max.
    b. it is measured in a specially equipped laboratory.
    c. the test for it measures carbon dioxide used at maximal exercise intensities.
    d. it is measured using a treadmill test.

3. All of the following are true regarding maximal heart rate EXCEPT:
    a. to obtain a target heart rate, divide by the desired percentage of maximal heart rate.
    b. the formula is 220 minus your age.
    c. it refers to the heart rate at which the highest level of oxygen consumption occurs.
    d. it is a way to estimate VO_2 max that does not require a laboratory.

4. When we are inactive _____, supplies/supply between 85 and 90% of the total amount of energy needed by muscles.
    a. amino acids
    b. carbohydrates
    c. fat
    d. glucose

5. A good exercise to work the arms and shoulders is:
    a. abdominal curls.
    b. stair climbing.
    c. leg lifts.
    d. push-ups.

6. All of the following are true regarding a personal fitness program EXCEPT:
    a. it should include activities you enjoy.
    b. benefits of training diminish within 8 months after training stops.
    c. it should include resistance training.
    d. it should include aerobic training.

7. All of the following are true regarding fitness in America EXCEPT:
    a. 40% of adults do not achieve recommended levels of physical activity.
    b. 40% of adults are inactive.
    c. 9 in 10 public schools require students to participate in physical activity.
    d. schools are encouraged to include physical activity as a daily part of the curriculum.

8. Endurance refers to:
    a. the level of maximum force that muscles can produce.
    b. the length of time muscles can perform physical activities.
    c. a person's range of motion.
    d. an increased sense of well-being.

144

9. All of the following are examples of an improved sense of well-being resulting from regular physical activity EXCEPT:
   a. increased anxiety.
   b. decreased stress.
   c. decreased risk of dementia.
   d. decreased depression.

10. Who benefits from regular physical activity?
    a. Everyone except the elderly
    b. Children but not adolescents
    c. Almost everyone
    d. Adults only

11. All of the following are true regarding exercise and body weight EXCEPT:
    a. increased muscle mass increases caloric requirements.
    b. combined with a stable caloric intake, it can lead to a small weight loss.
    c. it helps people lose body fat.
    d. in order to lose weight, exercise must be combined with drastic calorie reductions.

12. The health of the body as measured by muscular strength, endurance, and flexibility is called:
    a. physical fitness.
    b. aerobic fitness.
    c. flexibility.
    d. stamina.

13. A state of respiratory and circulatory health as measured by the ability to deliver oxygen to muscles and the capacity of muscles to use the oxygen for physical activity is called:
    a. physical fitness.
    b. aerobic fitness.
    c. flexibility.
    d. stamina.

14. All of the following describe maximal oxygen consumption EXCEPT:
    a. it is the highest amount of oxygen that can be delivered to muscles for physical activity.
    b. it is the highest amount of oxygen that can be used by muscles for physical activity.
    c. it is abbreviated MHR.
    d. it is also called maximal volume of oxygen.

15. All of the following are true regarding physical activity EXCEPT:
    a. obese people can be fit.
    b. thin people can be unfit.
    c. it is measured by strength, endurance, and flexibility.
    d. a person only needs one of the following to be fit: strength, endurance, or flexibility.

16. Strength refers to:
    a. the level of maximum force that muscles can produce.
    b. the length of time muscles can perform physical activities.
    c. a person's range of motion.
    d. an increased sense of well-being.

17. Flexibility refers to:
    a. the level of maximum force that muscles can produce.
    b. the length of time muscles can perform physical activities.
    c. a person's range of motion.
    d. an increased sense of well-being.

18. In order to increase muscle strength people should:
    a. lift lighter weights and push against them repeatedly.
    b. lift heavy weights.
    c. do yoga.
    d. stretch.

19. In order to increase muscle endurance people should:
    a. lift lighter weights and push against them repeatedly.
    b. lift heavy weights.
    c. do yoga.
    d. stretch.

20. All of the following are true regarding stamina EXCEPT:
    a. it is affected by conditioning.
    b. it is affected by inherited traits.
    c. it refers to the extent of one's ability to deliver and use oxygen in organs.
    d. it refers to the extent of one's ability to deliver and use oxygen in muscles.

21. All of the following are true regarding diet and exercise EXCEPT:
    a. the foods you eat serve as a source of energy for physical activity.
    b. the body needs fat as a primary energy source.
    c. the quality of your diet rarely affects your physical fitness.
    d. the body needs glucose as a primary energy source.

22. Muscles use all of the following for energy EXCEPT:
    a. amino acids.
    b. glucose.
    c. fats.
    d. phytochemicals.

23. All of the following are true regarding aerobic activities EXCEPT:
    a. this term refers to low- to moderate-intensity activities.
    b. fat is the primary fuel source.
    c. oxygen is required to convert fat into energy.
    d. aerobic means "without oxygen."

24. High-intensity, short-duration activities are fueled primarily by:
    a. glucose.
    b. fat.
    c. amino acids.
    d. glycerol.

146

25. All of the following are true regarding anaerobic activities EXCEPT:
    a. sprinting is an example.
    b. anaerobic means "with oxygen."
    c. glucose is the primary fuel.
    d. the glucose supply comes from stored glycogen.

26. A healthful diet for physical activity includes all of the following EXCEPT:
    a. a variety of fruits and vegetables.
    b. whole-grain products.
    c. protein powders and amino acid supplements.
    d. lean meats and low-fat dairy products.

27. All of the following are true regarding water intake and exercise EXCEPT:
    a. physical activity increases the body's need for water.
    b. hot and humid climates increase the body's need for water.
    c. the amount of water lost during exercise is equivalent to the amount of weight gained.
    d. urine should be pale yellow in color.

28. A good exercise to work the legs and buttocks is:
    a. pull-ups.
    b. push-ups.
    c. cycling.
    d. sit-ups.

29. The recommended levels of physical activity for Americans are:
    a. at least 2 hours and 30 minutes per week of moderate-intensity aerobic exercise.
    b. at least 1 hour and 30 minutes per week of moderate-intensity aerobic exercise.
    c. at least 7 sessions of strengthening activities per week.
    d. at least 2 sessions of strengthening activities per month.

30. All of the following groups of people should consult a physician prior to engaging in exercise EXCEPT:
    a. elite athletes.
    c. people over 40 years old.
    c. people with chronic diseases such as hypertension.
    d. people who are out of shape.

To check yourself, use the answer key at the bottom of the page.[28]

---

[28] 1. b, 2. c, 3. a, 4. c, 5. d, 6. b, 7. c, 8. b, 9. a, 10. c, 11. d, 12. a, 13. b, 14. c, 15. d, 16. a, 17. c, 18. b, 19. a, 20. c, 21. c, 22. d, 23. d, 24. a, 25. b, 26. c, 27. c 28. c, 29. a, 30. a

Unit 28 – Nutrition and Physical Performance

Key Concepts

- Endurance is affected by genetics, training, and nutrition.
- Glycogen stores and endurance can be increased by diet and training.
- Abnormal or absent menstrual cycles in female athletes should not be dismissed but corrected with increased caloric intake.
- Glucose and fat are used as energy sources during exercise but in different proportions.
- Intense physical activity is primarily fueled by glucose, and fats are the main source of energy for low- to moderate-intensity exercise.
- A few ergogenic aids that claim to improve performance work to some extent, but most do not.

Unit Outline

I. Sports nutrition
   A. Basic components of energy formation during exercise
      1. Anaerobic energy formation
      2. Aerobic energy formation
II. Nutrition and physical performance
   A. Glycogen stores and performance
      1. Carbohydrate loading
         a. Carbohydrate-loading caveats
   B. Protein need
      1. Protein and amino acid supplements
      2. Pre-event, event, and recovery foods
         a. Pre-event foods and fluids
         b. Event floods and fluids
         c. Post-event foods and fluids
   C. Hydration
      1. Maintaining hydration status during exercise
         a. Fluids that don't hydrate
         b. Estimating fluid needs: Sweat rate
      2. Dehydration: The consequences
      3. Hyponatremia and excess water
   D. Body fat and weight: Heavy issues for athletes
      1. Exercise, body fat, and health in women
      2. Wrestling: The sport of weight cycling
   E. Iron status of athletes
   F. Ergogenic aids: The athlete's dilemma
      1. The path to improved performance

Unit Glossary

- **glycogen:** The storage form of glucose. Glycogen is stored in muscles and the liver.
- **ergogenic aids** (ergo = work; genic = producing): Substances that increase the capacity for muscular work.

148

- **ATP, ADP:** Adenosine triphosphate (ah-den-o-scene tri-phos-fate) and adenosine diphosphate. Molecules containing a form of phosphorous that can trap energy obtained from the macronutrients. ADP becomes ATP when it traps energy and returns to being ADP when it releases energy for muscular and other work.
- **electrolytes:** Minerals such as sodium and potassium that carry a charge when in solution. Many electrolytes help the body maintain an appropriate amount of fluid.
- **hydration status:** The state of the adequacy of fluid in the body tissues. Dehydration indicates the presence of inadequate fluid in body tissues, and hyperhydration means there is too much.
- **hyponatremia:** A deficiency of sodium in the blood (135 mmol/L sodium or less).
- **sweat rate:** Fluid loss per hour of exercise. It equals the sum of body weight loss plus fluid intake.

Practice Multiple-Choice Test

1. The two main substrates for energy formation in muscles are:
   a. glucose and fatty acids.
   b. glucose and amino acids.
   c. amino acids and fatty acids.
   d. glucose and glycerol.

2. The main source of energy for low- and moderate-intensity activity is:
   a. glycogen.
   b. fat.
   c. amino acids.
   d. proteins.

3. The main source of energy for high-intensity activity is:
   a. glycogen.
   b. fat.
   c. glycerol.
   d. amino acids.

4. How many grams of carbohydrate are in a 2000-calorie diet that provides 60% of total calories from carbohydrate?
   a. 240 grams
   b. 270 grams
   c. 300 grams
   d. 330 grams

5. All of the following are true regarding glycemic index EXCEPT:
   a. low-glycemic index foods prior to exercise appear to sustain glycogen stores.
   b. low-glycemic index foods may improve endurance.
   c. corn flakes, Gatorade, and potatoes are all low-glycemic index foods.
   d. high-glycemic index foods increase blood glucose levels.

6. All of the following are true regarding pre-exercise foods EXCEPT:
   a. meals providing protein and carbohydrates should be consumed 3-4 hours prior to the event.
   b. oatmeal sweetened with honey is a good pre-event meal choice.
   c. carbohydrates decrease blood insulin levels.
   d. meals should focus on nutrient-dense foods.

7. The amount of fluids athletes need during events can be estimated by calculating:
   a. urine loss rate.
   b. weight gain rate.
   c. sweat rate.
   d. thirst index.

8. A condition caused by low body water and sodium content due to excessive loss of water through sweat in hot weather is called:
   a. heat exhaustion.
   b. heat stroke.
   c. hyperhydration.
   d. hyponatremia.

9. Body fat levels should not be below _____ in male and _____ in female athletes:
   a. 3%, 15%
   b. 8%, 18%
   c. 5%, 12%
   d. 10%, 20%

10. All of the following are true regarding wrestling EXCEPT:
    a. "making weight" is a practice of drastic weight loss.
    b. wrestlers commonly lose weight 50 to 100 times over a high school or college career.
    c. weight cycling has been found to be safe.
    d. a minimum of 7% body fat is used to assign wrestlers to weight classes.

11. The storage form of glucose in the body is called:
    a. glucagon.
    b. glycogen.
    c. triglycerides.
    d. carbohydrates.

12. Glycogen is stored in the:
    a. kidney and liver.
    b. muscles and heart.
    c. muscles and liver.
    d. liver and heart.

13. All of the following factors affect physical performance EXCEPT:
    a. education.
    b. genetics.
    c. training.
    d. nutrition.

14. Ergogenic aids are:
    a. substances that are banned in professional sports leagues.
    b. substances that increase mental focus in sports.
    c. advice given by coaches to athletes.
    d. substances that increase the capacity for muscular work.

150

15. All of the following are true regarding anaerobic energy production EXCEPT:
    a. ATP is formed without oxygen.
    b. it generates most of the energy used for low-intensity muscular work.
    c. glucose from the liver and muscle glycogen are converted to ATP.
    d. glucose is converted to pyruvate during anaerobic energy production.

16. All of the following are true regarding aerobic energy production EXCEPT:
    a. the conversion of pyruvate and fatty acids to ATP requires oxygen.
    b. fatty acids are used to fuel low- and moderate-intensity exercise.
    c. less ATP is delivered by the breakdown of fatty acids than glucose.
    d. energy formation from fatty acids is unlimited in the presence of oxygen.

17. All of the following are true regarding electrolytes EXCEPT:
    a. sodium and potassium are examples.
    b. they are minerals that carry a charge in solution.
    c. they help the body maintain an appropriate amount of fluid.
    d. they are not related to energy formation and physical performance.

18. All of the following are true regarding carbohydrate loading EXCEPT:
    a. carbohydrates should be increased to 60 to 70% of calories for less than 24 hours prior to the event.
    b. it is used to increase muscle glycogen stores.
    c. carbohydrate loading benefits endurance athletes.
    d. carbohydrate loading should be done prior to running a 10K.

19. All of the following are true regarding recovery foods EXCEPT:
    a. protein intake after hard exercise appears to hasten recovery.
    b. protein and carbohydrate intake together decrease recovery time.
    c. antioxidants facilitate muscle repair.
    d. fluids are not a part of post-exercise recovery.

20. The state of adequacy of fluid in the body tissues is called:
    a. hydration status.
    b. dehydration.
    c. hyperhydration.
    d. hyponatremia.

21. Inadequate fluid in body tissues is called:
    a. hydration status.
    b. dehydration.
    c. hyperhydration.
    d. hyponatremia.

22. A deficiency of sodium in the blood (135 mmol/L sodium or less) is called:
    a. hydration status.
    b. dehydration.
    c. hyperhydration.
    d. hyponatremia.

23. All of the following are recommendations for maintaining hydration status during exercise EXCEPT:
    a. for short events, drink 2 cups of water one to two hours before the event.
    b. for long events, drink a beverage that contains sodium and carbohydrates.
    c. for all activities, water should be consumed at regular intervals.
    d. fluids high in sugar and alcoholic beverages are effective at maintaining hydration.

24. A condition characterized by an internal body temperature of 105 degrees F due to prolonged exposure to heat and requiring emergency medical care is called:
    a. heat exhaustion.
    b. heat stroke.
    c. hyperhydration.
    d. hyponatremia.

25. All of the following are signs of dehydration EXCEPT:
    a. thirst.
    b. having chills when it is hot out.
    c. lightheadedness.
    d. increased concentration.

26. Which of the following ergogenic aids has been shown to reduce fatigue and improve endurance at low doses?
    a. Bee pollen
    b. Carnitine
    c. Caffeine
    d. Chromium picolinate

27. A popular type of ergogenic aid used by bodybuilders that has the adverse side effects of liver damage and increased LDL-cholesterol is:
    a. carnitine.
    b. anabolic steroids.
    c. boron.
    d. branched-chain amino acids.

28. An ergogenic aid that has been shown to increase peak muscle force in short, high-intensity exercises is:
    a. EPO.
    b. glycerol.
    c. GBL.
    d. creatine.

29. All of the following are true regarding excessive use of protein powders EXCEPT:
    a. muscle mass and strength increase.
    b. dehydration is an adverse effect.
    c. it can result in liver problems.
    d. it can result in kidney problems.

30. The most common nutrient deficiency among athletes is:
    a. iron.
    b. vitamin C.
    c. magnesium.
    d. potassium.

152

To check yourself, use the answer key at the bottom of the page.[29]

---

[29] 1. a, 2. b, 3. a, 4. c, 5. c, 6. c, 7. c, 8. a, 9. c, 10. c, 11. b, 12. c, 13. a, 14. d, 15. b, 16. c, 17. d, 18. a, 19. d, 20. a, 21. b, 22. d, 23. d, 24. b, 25. d, 26. c, 27. b, 28. d, 29. a, 30. a

Unit 29 – Good Nutrition for Life: Pregnancy, Breastfeeding, and Infancy

Key Concepts

- There are no "maternal instincts" that draw women to select and consume a good diet during pregnancy.
- The fetus is not a parasite.
- Fetal and infant growth are characterized by "critical periods" during which all essential nutrients needed for growth and development must be available or growth and development will not proceed normally.
- An adult's risk of certain chronic diseases may be partially determined by maternal nutrition during pregnancy and the person's own nutrition early in life.
- Breast-feeding is the optimal method of feeding infants.
- Rates of growth and development are higher during infancy than at any other time in life.

Unit Outline

I. A healthy start
    A. Unhealthy starts on life
    B. Improving the health of U.S. infants
II. Nutrition and pregnancy
    A. Critical periods
    B. The fetal origins hypothesis
        1. The fetus is not a parasite
    C. Prepregnancy weight status and prenatal weight gain are important
        1. What's the right amount of weight to gain during pregnancy?
        2. Where does the weight gain go?
        3. Where does the weight gain go—after pregnancy?
    D. The need for calories and key nutrients during pregnancy
        1. Calories
        2. Folate
        3. Vitamin A
        4. Calcium
        5. Vitamin D
        6. Iron
        7. Iodine
        8. EPA and DHA
    E. What's a good diet for pregnancy?
        1. Why alcohol and pregnancy don't mix
        2. Vitamin and mineral supplements
    F. Teen pregnancy
III. Breast-feeding
    A. What's so special about breast milk?
    B. Is breast-feeding best for all new mothers and infants?
IV. How breast-feeding works
    A. Breast milk production
    B. Nutrition and breast-feeding
        1. Calorie and nutrient needs
        2. What's a good diet for breast-feeding women?
        3. Are supplements recommended for breast-feeding women?
        4. Dietary cautions for breast-feeding women

V. Infant nutrition
   A. Infant growth
      1. Growth charts for infants
      2. Body composition changes with growth
   B. Nutrition and mental development
VI. Infant feeding recommendations
   A. Introducing solid foods
   B. Foods to avoid
   C. Do infants need supplements?
   D. The development of healthy eating habits begins in infancy
      1. Teaching infants the right lessons about food
   E. Making feeding time pleasurable

Unit Glossary

- **infant morality rate:** Deaths that occur within the first year of life per 1,000 live births.
- **low-birthweight infants:** Infants weighting less than 2500 grams (5.5 pounds) at birth.
- **preterm infants:** Infants born at or before 37 weeks of gestation (pregnancy).
- **fetus:** A baby in the womb from the eighth week of pregnancy until birth. (Before then, it is referred to as an embryo.)
- **growth:** A process characterized by increases in cell number and size.
- **development:** Processes involved in enhancing functional capabilities. For example, the brain grows, but the ability to reason develops.
- **critical period:** A specific interval of time during which cells of a tissue or organ are genetically programmed to multiply. If the supply of nutrients needed for cell multiplication is not available during the specific time interval, the growth and development of the tissue or organ are permanently impaired.
- **trimester:** One-third of the normal duration of pregnancy. The first trimester is 0 to 13 weeks, the second is 13 to 26 weeks, and the third is 26 to 40 weeks.
- **neural tube defects:** Malformations of the spinal cord and brain. They are among the most common and severe fetal malformations, occurring in approximately one in every 1000 pregnancies. Neural tube defects include spina bifida (spinal cord fluid protrudes through a gap in the spinal cord), anencephaly (absence of the brain or spinal cord), and encephalocele (protrusion of the brain through the skull).
- **colostrum:** The milk produced during the first few days after delivery. It contains more antibodies, protein, and certain minerals than the mature milk that is produced later. It is thicker than mature milk and has a yellowish color.

Practice Multiple-Choice Test

1. Low-birthweight infants weigh:
   a. less than 5.5 pounds at birth.
   b. less than 3 pounds at birth.
   c. less than 7 pounds at birth.
   d. less than 2 pounds at birth.

2. All of the following are true regarding infant mortality rate EXCEPT:
   a. the U.S. ranks 29th among countries of the world.
   b. low birth weight contributes to infant mortality.
   c. infants born preterm have a higher infant mortality rate.
   d. it is defined as deaths that occur within the first 2 years of life per 1000 live births.

3. At what week in pregnancy is an embryo now considered a fetus?
   a. Tenth
   b. Eighth
   c. Twelfth
   d. Sixth

4. Women of normal weight (BMI 18.5-24.9) should gain _____ pounds during pregnancy.
   a. 28-40
   b. 25-35
   c. 15-25
   d. 11-20

5. The only supplement recommended for all pregnant women is:
   a. calcium.
   b. vitamin D.
   c. iodine.
   d. iron.

6. All of the following are true regarding folate EXCEPT:
   a. deficiency is associated with fetal growth failure.
   b. deficiency is linked to neural tube defects.
   c. it is considered an "at risk" nutrient during pregnancy.
   d. 400 micrograms of folate per day should be consumed prior to and during pregnancy.

7. Dietary recommendations for pregnancy include all of the following EXCEPT:
   a. "Do not drink alcoholic beverages."
   b. "Consume sufficient fiber."
   c. "Limit coffee to six or fewer cups a day."
   d. "Consume sufficient calories for adequate weight gain."

8. All of the following are true regarding breast milk EXCEPT:
   a. it may protect against the development of cancer of the lymph system.
   b. it is a complete source of nutrition for the first year of life.
   c. IQ in breast-fed babies tends to be higher.
   d. it contains essential and nonessential fats.

9. Processes involved in enhancing functional capacities such as the ability to reason are called:
   a. development.
   b. intervals.
   c. growth.
   d. maturation.

10. A process characterized by increases in cell number and size is called:
    a. development.
    b. intervals.
    c. growth.
    d. maturing.

156

11. Preterm infants are infants born:
    a. at or before 40 weeks of gestation.
    b. at or before 39 weeks of gestation.
    c. at or before 38 weeks of gestation.
    d. at or before 37 weeks of gestation.

12. All of the following are true regarding critical periods EXCEPT:
    a. a critical period is an interval of time when cells are genetically programmed to multiply.
    b. sufficient nutrients must be available for cell multiplication to occur.
    c. if nutrients are not available the developing organ will be impaired.
    d. if nutrients become available after the critical period the organs will grow to full size.

13. All of the following are major factors that directly influence birthweight EXCEPT:
    a. duration of pregnancy.
    b. postnatal weight loss.
    c. smoking.
    d. prepregnancy weight status.

14. All of the following describe the "fetal origins" hypothesis EXCEPT:
    a. gene functions may be modified by excessive supplies of nutrients during pregnancy.
    b. gene functions may be modified by inadequate supplies of nutrients during pregnancy.
    c. susceptibility to chronic diseases later in life may be influenced by maternal nutrition.
    d. high maternal intake in the last months of pregnancy may increase the risk of diabetes development.

15. Underweight women (BMI <18) should gain _____ pounds during pregnancy.
    a. 28-40
    b. 25-35
    c. 15-25
    d. 15-20

16. Overweight women (BMI 25-29.9) should gain _____ pounds during pregnancy.
    a. 28-40
    b. 24-35
    c. 15-25
    d. 11-20

17. During the second trimester, women need, on average, _____ additional calories per day.
    a. 450
    b. 340
    c. 500
    d. 1000

18. During the third trimester, women need, on average, _____ additional calories per day.
    a. 450
    b. 340
    c. 500
    d. 1000

19. All of the following are true regarding vitamin A intake and pregnancy EXCEPT:
    a. too little is associated with poor fatal growth.
    b. too much in the form of retinol supplements can cause fetal malformations.
    c. pregnant women should limit their intake of beta-carotene to <5000 IU per day.
    d. pregnant women should limit their intake of retinol to <5000 IU per day.

20. The most common nutrient deficiency in pregnant women is:
    a. calcium.
    b. iron.
    c. iodine.
    d. vitamin A.

21. All of the following are true regarding EPA and DHA EXCEPT:
    a. they are omega-3 fatty acids.
    b. they support development of vision in the fetus.
    c. most pregnant and breast-feeding women in the U.S. consume the recommended amount.
    d. good sources are fish, fish oils, and seafood.

22. All of the following are true regarding colostrum EXCEPT:
    a. it is the milk produced during the first days after delivery.
    b. it contains more antibodies than mature milk.
    c. it contains less protein than mature milk.
    d. it is thicker than mature milk.

23. All of the following are dietary recommendations for breastfeeding women EXCEPT:
    a. routine use of vitamin and mineral supplements is recommended.
    b. at least 14 cups of fluids should be consumed per day.
    c. alcohol intake should be avoided.
    d. caloric intake should not fall below 1500 calories per day.

24. All of the following are recommendations for feeding infants EXCEPT:
    a. exclusive breastfeeding for the first 6 months of life and continuing throughout the first year alongside other foods is best.
    b. at 8 months, solid foods should be introduced.
    c. breast-fed infants receiving little sun exposure should be given a vitamin D supplement.
    d. in infants, the first food should be iron fortified, such as iron-fortified cereal.

25. Foods that may cause allergic reactions and should be avoided in the infant's first year of life include all of the following EXCEPT:
    a. cow's milk.
    b. nuts.
    c. apples.
    d. egg white.

26. Foods that may cause choking and should be avoided in the first year of life include all of the following EXCEPT:
    a. frankfurter pieces.
    b. hard candy.
    c. popcorn.
    d. banana pieces.

158

27. Which two supplements may be recommended for use during infancy?
    a. Iron and calcium
    b. Fluoride and calcium
    c. Fluoride and vitamin D
    d. Vitamin D and calcium

28. Recommendations for feeding infants are based on all of the following EXCEPT:
    a. parental convenience.
    b. developmental readiness for solid foods.
    c. energy needs.
    d. nutrient needs.

29. Mental development in infants is LEAST affected by which of the following factors?
    a. The mother's nutrient status after pregnancy
    b. The social environment in which they are raised
    c. The psychological environment in which they are raised
    d. Nutrition during the critical period of the first year of life

30. Infants graduate to adult-type foods at:
    a. 6 months of age.
    b. 9 months of age.
    c. 12 months of age.
    d. 24 months of age.

To check yourself, use the answer key at the bottom of the page.[30]

---

[30] 1. c, 2. d, 3. b, 4. b, 5. d, 6. d, 7. c, 8. b, 9. a, 10. c, 11. d, 12. d, 13. b, 14. d, 15. a, 16. c, 17. b, 18. a, 19. c, 20. b, 21. c, 22. c, 23. a, 24. b, 25. c, 26. d, 27. c, 28. a, 29. a, 30. c

Unit 30 – Nutrition for the Growing Years: Childhood through Adolescence

Key Concepts

- There is no evidence to support the notion that children are born knowing what foods they should eat.
- Children are born with regulatory processes that help them decide how much to eat.
- Parents and caretakers should decide *what* foods to offer children. Children should decide *how much* to eat.
- Diet and other behaviors of children and adolescents affect health before and during the adult years.

Unit Outline

I. The span of growth and development
   A. The nutritional foundation
   B. Characteristics of growth in children
      1. CDC's growth charts for children and adolescents
      2. Food jags and normal appetite changes
      3. Hunger can make kids irritable!
   C. The adolescent growth spurt
      1. Can you predict or influence adult height?
   D. Overweight and type 2 diabetes: Growing problems
      1. Causes of overweight in young people
      2. Medicalization of obesity and treatment
      3. Prevention of overweight
         a. Physical activity guidelines for children and adolescents
   E. How do food preferences develop?
   F. What's a good diet for children and adolescents?
      1. Recommendations for fat intake
      2. Is milk bad for children?
   G. Status of children's and adolescents' diets
   H. Early diet and later disease

Practice Multiple-Choice Test

1. All of the following are true regarding growth and development characteristics of one to two year olds EXCEPT:
   a. growth continues at a very high rate.
   b. baby teeth continue to appear.
   c. the child drinks from a cup.
   d. the child likes to eat with his or her hands.

2. All of the following are true regarding growth and development characteristics of two to three year olds EXCEPT:
   a. the child has all 20 teeth.
   b. there are slower gains in height and weight.
   c. the child does not associate hunger with need for food at this stage.
   d. the child at times has a favorite food.

3. All of the following are true regarding growth and development characteristics of nine to twelve year olds EXCEPT:
   a. permanent teeth appear.
   b. a growth spurt in girls usually appears.
   c. children are irritable when hungry.
   d. the child needs 8 hours of sleep.

4. All of the following are true regarding growth and development characteristics of fourteen to sixteen year olds EXCEPT:
   a. girls have achieved maximum growth.
   b. boys have achieved maximum growth.
   c. the youth has an enormous appetite.
   d. boys are in a growth spurt.

5. All of the following are true regarding growth spurts EXCEPT:
   a. prior to a growth spurt, appetite increases.
   b. prior to a growth spurt, food intake increases.
   c. children put on a few pounds of fat stores before a growth spurt.
   d. muscle stores are used to supply energy needed for growth in height.

6. All of the following are true regarding growth charts for children and adolescents EXCEPT:
   a. the American Pediatric Society growth charts are used to monitor progress.
   b. charts are available for females and males from 0 to 36 months.
   c. charts are available for females and males from 2 to 20 years.
   d. the Centers for Disease Control and Prevention growth charts are used to monitor progress.

7. The adolescent growth spurt of boys occurs between the ages of:
   a. 14 and 16 years.
   b. 7 and 8 years.
   c. 12 and 14 years.
   d. 9 and 12 years.

8. All of the following are true regarding the development of food choices EXCEPT:
   a. there is no direct evidence that food preferences (other than a preference for sweetness andn a dislike of bitterness) are inborn.
   b. children instinctively know what to eat.
   c. food preferences are highly individual.
   d. food likes and dislikes are almost entirely shaped by the environment.

9. All of the following are true regarding snacks EXCEPT:
   a. they serve as an important source of calories in the diets of children and teens.
   b. good choices include yogurt and cheese.
   c. they serve as an important source of nutrition in the diets of children and teens.
   d. good choices include soda, candy, and donuts.

10. All of the following are true regarding milk intake in children and teens EXCEPT:
    a. it is not recommended because humans were not meant to drink milk.
    b. it serves as an important source of calcium.
    c. children who drink milk have higher bone density.
    d. 2-3 servings of milk and dairy products per day are recommended.

11. Good nutrition is important during the growing years for all of the following reasons EXCEPT:
    a. growth will not proceed normally unless energy is adequate.
    b. growth will not proceed normally unless nutrients are adequate.
    c. early diets do not influence risk for chronic disease later in life.
    d. food preferences develop during the growing years.

12. All of the following are true regarding growth and development characteristics of three to four year olds EXCEPT:
    a. the child gains 4-6 pounds.
    b. the child feeds herself/himself.
    c. the child drinks from a cup.
    d. the child grows about 6-8 inches.

13. All of the following are true regarding growth and development characteristics of five to six year olds EXCEPT:
    a. the child's legs lengthen.
    b. the child prefers spicy foods.
    c. the child begins to lose front baby teeth.
    d. the permanent molars appear.

14. All of the following are true regarding growth and development characteristics of six to nine year olds EXCEPT:
    a. gains in height slow.
    b. gains in weight slow.
    c. the child sleeps 5 to 6 hours.
    d. the child is likely to have childhood communicable diseases.

15. All of the following are true regarding growth and development characteristics of twelve to fourteen year olds EXCEPT:
    a. appetite decreases.
    b. a growth spurt in boys begins.
    c. menstruation in girls begins.
    d. there are wide differences in height and weight of either sex of the same age.

16. Growth charts for 2 to 20 year olds consist of graphs of all of the following EXCEPT:
    a. weight for age.
    b. head circumference.
    c. height (stature) for age.
    d. weight for height.

17. All of the following are true regarding growth charts for 2 to 20 year olds EXCEPT:
    a. percentiles reflect the distribution of measures in a representative sample.
    b. children in the highest percentile ranges should be evaluated for nutrition and health problems.
    c. children in the lowest percentile ranges should be evaluated for nutrition and health problems.
    d. a child between the 50th and 75th percentiles is similar to 50% of children in that range.

18. All of the following are true regarding BMI and children and adolescents EXCEPT:
    a. BMI increases with age in children and adolescents.
    b. ranges to classify BMI in children and adolescents are the same as those used for adults.
    c. BMI must be calculated in order to use the charts.
    d. A BMI that is very high for age is considered a potential health problem.

162

19. All of the following are true regarding "food jags" EXCEPT:
    a. parents should worry about food jags.
    b. children may insist on eating only a few favorite foods.
    c. when growth is not occurring interest in food decreases.
    d. fluctuations in appetite and food intake are normal.

20. Body mass index is a measure of:
    a. height for age.
    b. weight for age.
    c. weight for height.
    d. weight for frame size.

21. Irritability in children who are usually well mannered is often an indication of:
    a. being spoiled.
    b. bad behavior.
    c. hunger.
    d. poor manners.

22. The adolescent growth spurt of girls occurs between the ages of:
    a. 14 and 16 years.
    b. 7 and 8 years.
    c. 12 and 14 years.
    d. 9 and 12 years.

23. All of the following are true regarding growth spurts EXCEPT:
    a. teenagers gain approximately 50% of their adult weight.
    b. teenagers gain approximately 20 to 25% of adult height.
    c. girls gain on average 18 pounds, and boys, 20 pounds.
    d. teenagers gain 90% of their total bone mass.

24. All of the following are true regarding influences on height EXCEPT:
    a. there are supplements and special diets available that can increase height.
    b. children tend to achieve a height between the heights of their biological parents.
    c. a healthy birthweight supports growth in height.
    d. adequate nutrition supports growth in height.

25. All of the following are true regarding type 2 diabetes in children and adolescents EXCEPT:
    a. it is estimated that 4% of children and adolescents have impaired glucose tolerance.
    b. the rise in type 2 diabetes is primarily attributed to genetic changes.
    c. it is estimated that 6 to 17% of overweight children and adolescents have type 2 diabetes.
    d. diabetes worsens with time and causes long-term health impairments.

26. All of the following are true regarding overweight in children and adolescents EXCEPT:
    a. rates have risen remarkably since the 1960s.
    b. overweight-related disorders are on the rise.
    c. approximately 90% of overweight children have risk factors for cardiovascular disease.
    d. one way to prevent overweight is to make sure children engage in moderate- to vigorous-intensity exercise for an hour every day.

27. All of the following are causes of overweight in children and adolescents EXCEPT:
    a. "obesigenic" trends have developed over the last 20-30 years.
    b. children and adolescents have fewer opportunities for physical activity.
    c. children eat larger amounts of fruits and vegetables than 20 years ago.
    d. processes that regulate appetite are being overridden by environmental conditions.

28. Prevention of overweight in children and adolescents should include all of the following EXCEPT:
    a. stomach stapling.
    b. increased opportunities for physical activity.
    c. a wider array of healthy food choices in schools.
    d. a wider array of healthy food choices at home.

29. Dietary recommendations for the growing years include all of the following EXCEPT:
    a. boiled, broiled, and baked foods should be consumed more than fried foods.
    b. whole-grain foods should be eaten.
    c. snacks should not be given to children and adolescents.
    d. fat intakes should be in the range of 25% to 35% of total calories.

30. All of the following are true regarding the status of children's and adolescents' diets EXCEPT:
    a. they consume too little fiber.
    b. 49% meet recommendations for whole grains, fruits, and vegetables.
    c. they consume too little calcium.
    d. they consume too little vitamin D, folate, and potassium.

To check yourself, use the answer key at the bottom of the page.[31]

---

[31] 1. a, 2. c, 3. d, 4. b, 5. d, 6. a, 7. c, 8. b, 9. d, 10. a, 11. c, 12. d, 13. b, 14. c, 15. a, 16. b, 17. d, 18. b, 19. a, 20. c, 21. c, 22. d, 23. d, 24. a, 25. b, 26. c, 27. c, 28. a, 29. c, 30. b

Unit 31 – Nutrition and Health Maintenance for Adults of All Ages

Key Concepts

- Age does not necessarily predict health status. Healthy adults come in all ages.
- Dietary intake, body weight, and physical activity influence changes in health status with age.
- Aging processes begin at the cellular level.
- Medications, diseases, and biological processes associated with aging influence adults' requirements for certain essential nutrients.

Unit Outline

I.   You never outgrow your need for a good diet
II. The age wave
    A. Why the gains in life expectancy?
    B. Living in the bonus round: Diet and life expectancy
        1. Physical activity and longevity
    C. Calorie restriction and longevity
III. Nutrition issues for adults of all ages
    A. Breaking the chains of chronic disease development
    B. Nutrient needs of middle-aged and older adults
        1. Fluid needs
        2. Does taste change with age?
    C. Psychological and social aspects of nutrition in older adults
    D. Eating right during middle age and the older years

Unit Glossary

- **life expectancy:** The average length of life of people of a given age.

Practice Multiple-Choice Test

1. Which of the following statements regarding life expectancy in the United States is true?
    a. The proportion of people aged 65 years and older is increasing.
    b. By the year 2050, approximately 50% of the U.S. population will be 65 years or older.
    c. Since 1990, life expectancy has increased by 63%.
    d. The United States ranks twentieth in life expectancy worldwide.

2. All of the following are true regarding life expectancy in the United States EXCEPT:
    a. it varies by sex and race.
    b. African American men have the shortest life expectancy.
    c. Caucasian men have the longest life expectancy.
    d. life expectancy for females exceeds that of males.

3. All of the following are characteristics of diets of adults with low disease rates and increased longevity EXCEPT:
    a. breakfast consumption.
    b. regular physical activity.
    c. social isolation.
    d. above-average intake of whole-grain products.

4. A nutritional consequence of lowered stomach acidity is:
   a. decreased absorption of vitamins B_{12} and C.
   b. reduced caloric need.
   c. increased dietary requirement for vitamin D.
   d. dehydration risk.

5. A nutritional consequence of reduced production of vitamin D in the skin is:
   a. decreased absorption of vitamins B_{12} and C.
   b. reduced caloric need.
   c. increased dietary requirement for vitamin D.
   d. dehydration risk.

6. MyPyramid recommendations for 45 year olds include all of the following EXCEPT:
   a. 6-9 ounces of grains.
   b. 3.5-4 cups of vegetables.
   c. 3 cups of milk.
   d. 2 cups of fruits.

7. MyPyramid recommendations for 75 year olds include all of the following EXCEPT:
   a. 2 cups of milk.
   b. 1.5-2 cups of fruits.
   c. 6-7 ounces of grains.
   d. 5-6 ounces of meats.

8. Which of the following senses decreases the LEAST with aging?
   a. Sense of sight
   b. Sense of hearing
   c. Sense of smell
   d. Sense of taste

9. All of the following are reasons for good nutrition during the adult years EXCEPT:
   a. it improves overall sense of well-being.
   b. it delays the onset of certain chronic diseases.
   c. it decreases years of life.
   d. it helps adults feel vigorous as they age.

10. All of the following are true regarding the process of aging EXCEPT:
    a. aging is a disease.
    b. aging cannot be prevented.
    c. the causes of many diseases are unrelated to aging.
    d. diets high is saturated fats and low in fruits and vegetables are linked to disease development.

11. The average length of life of people of a given age is called:
    a. biological age.
    b. functional age.
    c. chronological age.
    d. life expectancy.

12. All of the following are true regarding the difference in life expectancy between males and females EXCEPT:
    a. it is largely related to behaviors.
    b. women tend to neglect their health more than males.
    c. men tend to pay less attention to what they eat than females.
    d. men tend to consume more alcoholic beverages than females.

13. All of the following are true regarding the gains in life expectancy EXCEPT:
    a. infant deaths have increased, which supports survival of the fittest.
    b. deaths from infectious diseases have decreased.
    c. nutrition has improved.
    d. advances have been made in medicine.

14. All of the following are true regarding gains in life expectancy EXCEPT:
    a. in 1900, 1 in 10 newborns died in the first year of life, and today it is less than 1 in 100.
    b. the mass use of vaccines has prevented diphtheria in infants and children.
    c. changes in genetics within the population as a whole have increased life expectancy.
    d. medical treatments and surgical advancements have added to the life expectancy.

15. All of the following are true regarding longevity EXCEPT:
    a. genetic background affects life span.
    b. environmental factors affect life span.
    c. children of long-lived parents live longer.
    d. people with inherited traits for high LDL cholesterol tend to live longer.

16. All of the following are characteristics of diets of adults with low disease rates and longer lives EXCEPT:
    a. regular consumption of fruits and vegetables.
    b. average intake of whole-grain products.
    c. lower-than-average consumption of saturated fats.
    d. alcohol in moderation.

17. A nutritional consequence of decreased lean muscle mass is:
    a. decreased absorption of vitamins B_{12} and C.
    b. reduced caloric need.
    c. increased dietary requirement for vitamin D.
    d. dehydration risk.

18. A nutritional consequence of decreased sensation of thirst is:
    a. decreased absorption of vitamins B_{12} and C.
    b. reduced caloric need.
    c. increased dietary requirement for vitamin D.
    d. dehydration risk.

19. All of the following are true regarding calorie restriction and longevity EXCEPT:
    a. animals fed diets providing 30% fewer calories than normal live longer.
    b. human studies have demonstrated that calorie restriction increases longevity.
    c. longevity increases may be related to reduced metabolic rate.
    d. longevity increases may be related to decreased aging processes.

20. MyPyramid recommendations for 75 year olds differ from those of 45 year olds in:
    a. decreased ounces of grains.
    b. increased teaspoons of oils.
    c. increased cups of milk.
    d. increased cups of fruits.

21. All of the following are true regarding physical activity and calorie needs of middle-aged and older adults EXCEPT:
    a. people who remain physically active maintain muscle mass.
    b. people who remain active experience less muscle and bone pain.
    c. people who remain active gain the same amount of body fat as those who are inactive.
    d. calorie needs will not decrease as much if people remain physically active.

22. The chain of chronic disease development can be shortened by all of the following EXCEPT:
    a. stabilizing weight during the adult years.
    b. following the Dietary Guidelines.
    c. regular intake of antioxidants from supplements.
    d. above-average intakes of fruits and vegetables.

23. All of the following are true regarding nutrient needs of middle-aged and older adults EXCEPT:
    a. caloric needs decrease.
    b. need for protein increases.
    c. need for vitamin C increases.
    d. need for calcium decreases.

24. All of the following are true regarding nutrient needs of middle-aged and older adults EXCEPT:
    a. fluid needs increase.
    b. need for vitamin D decreases.
    c. need for vitamin B_{12} increases.
    d. need for calcium increases.

25. All of the following are true regarding fluid needs in older adults EXCEPT:
    a. approximately 1 million elderly men and women are admitted to hospitals for dehydration each year.
    b. older people on limited budgets become dehydrated because they cannot afford as many beverages.
    c. many older people do not get thirsty when low on fluids.
    d. fluid needs can be met through the consumption of water.

26. Fluid needs for women of all ages are _____ per day.
    a. 11 cups of water from fluids and foods
    b. 8 cups of water from fluids and foods
    c. 15 cups of water from fluids and foods
    d. 20 cups of water from fluids and foods

27. Fluid needs for men of all ages are _____ per day.
    a. 11 cups of water from fluids and foods
    b. 8 cups of water from fluids and foods
    c. 15 cups of water from fluids and foods
    d. 20 cups of water from fluids and foods

28. All of the following are true regarding sense of taste and aging EXCEPT:
    a. the sense of taste does not decline to the extent that foods do not taste good.
    b. taste sensitivity diminishes slightly.
    c. taste sensitivity diminishes drastically.
    d. older people can taste almost the same as younger people.

29. All of the following are recommendations for a diet during middle and old age EXCEPT:
    a. "Drastically restrict calories."
    b. "Select nutrient-dense foods."
    c. "Emphasize low-fat dairy products."
    d. "Eat adequate fiber."

30. All of the following are recommendations for a diet during middle and old age EXCEPT:
    a. "Alterations may be necessary to reduce risk for chronic disease development."
    b. "Foods that are low in saturated fat should be chosen."
    c. "Adequate fluids should be obtained."
    d. "The diet does not influence longevity, so any choice is fine."

To check yourself, use the answer key at the bottom of the page.[32]

---

[32] 1. a, 2. c, 3. c, 4. a, 5. c, 6. b, 7. a, 8. d, 9. c, 10. a, 11. d, 12. b, 13. a, 14. c, 15. d, 16. b, 17. b, 18. d, 19. b, 20. a, 21. c, 22. c, 23. d, 24. b, 25. b, 26. a, 27. c, 28. c, 29. a, 30. d

Unit 32 – The Multiple Dimensions of Food Safety

Key Concepts

- The leading food safety problem in America is contamination of food by bacteria and viruses.
- Foodborne illnesses primarily result from unsafe methods of producing, storing, and handling food.
- Foodborne illnesses are linked to hundreds of foods but most commonly to raw and undercooked meats and eggs, shellfish, and unpasteurized milk.
- Most cases of foodborne illness are preventable.

Unit Outline

I. Threats to the safety of the food supply
    A. How good foods go bad
    B. Cross-contamination of foods
    C. Antibiotics, hormones, and other substances in foods
        1. Antibiotic resistance
        2. Hormones
        3. Pesticides and PCBs
    D. Causes and consequences of foodborne illness
        1. *Salmonella*
        2. *Campylobacter*
        3. *E. coli*
        4. Noroviruses
    E. Other causes of foodborne illnesses
        1. Foodborne illnesses related to seafoods
        2. Mercury contamination
        3. Ciguatera
        4. Red tide
        5. Botulism
        6. Parasites
        7. Mad cow disease
II. Preventing foodborne illnesses
    A. Food safety regulations
        1. Irradiation of foods
    B. The consumer's role in preventing foodborne illnesses
        1. Food safety basics
            a. There's a right way to wash your hands
            b. Keep hot foods hot and cold foods cold
            c. Don't eat raw milk, eggs, or meats
        2. Food handling and storage
        3. The safety of canned foods
III. There is a limit to what the consumer can do

Unit Glossary

- **foodborne illness:** An illness related to consumption of foods or beverages containing disease-causing bacteria, viruses, parasites, toxins, or other contaminants.

Practice Multiple-Choice Test

1. An illness related to consumption of food or beverages containing disease-causing bacteria, viruses, toxins, or other contaminants is called:
   a. spoiled food disease.
   b. indigestion.
   c. foodborne illness.
   d. stomach flu.

2. All of the following are true regarding cross-contamination of foods EXCEPT:
   a. microorganisms can contaminate safe food during processing.
   b. failure to wash cutting boards between the preparation of different raw foods is a major route.
   c. microorganisms can contaminate safe food during shipping.
   d. washing hands for 5 seconds in cold water can prevent cross-contamination.

3. All of the following are true regarding pesticides EXCEPT:
   a. use of DDT on insects was phased out 20 years ago.
   b. use of PCBs was phased out due to links with cancer.
   c. health problems appear in most population groups.
   d. chemical residues still remain in the environment.

4. All of the following are true regarding *Salmonella* EXCEPT:
   a. it is spread through human feces on food.
   b. undercooked seafood is a food commonly affected.
   c. symptoms are diarrhea, abdominal pain, and chills.
   d. onset is in 1-3 days.

5. All of the following are true regarding noroviruses EXCEPT:
   a. the usual source of contamination is human feces in oyster beds.
   b. undercooked seafood is a food commonly affected.
   c. symptoms include nausea, vomiting, and diarrhea.
   d. onset is in 30 days.

6. Seafood is a potential source of foodborne illness for all of the following reasons EXCEPT:
   a. seafood can be contaminated with mercury.
   b. fish contains omega-3 fatty acids.
   c. fish can carry ciguatera poisoning.
   d. shellfish can be contaminated with "red tide."

7. All of the following are true regarding *C. botulinum* EXCEPT:
   a. the bacteria need oxygen to thrive.
   b. it is one of the deadliest toxins.
   c. improperly canned goods are a source.
   d. airtight containers that have bulges may carry the toxin and their contents should not be eaten.

8. All of the following are true regarding proper hand washing EXCEPT:
   a. you should use cold water.
   b. you should scrub up to your elbows.
   c. it takes about 20 seconds to sanitize your hands.
   d. the crevices between your fingers and under your fingernails should be scrubbed.

9. Most bacteria grow rapidly between _____.
    a. 30 and 130 degrees F
    b. 50 and 150 degrees F
    c. 40 and 135 degrees F
    d. 40 and 150 degrees F

10. All of the following are true regarding safe handling of foods EXCEPT:
    a. you should keep hot foods hot.
    b. you should keep cold foods cold.
    c. freezing kills all bacteria.
    d. once frozen foods are thawed they can become contaminated with bacteria.

11. The Centers for Disease Control and Prevention (CDC) estimates all of the following related to foodborne illness EXCEPT:
    a. it causes sickness in 76 million people each year.
    b. it causes 325,000 hospitalizations each year.
    c. it causes over 5000 deaths each year.
    d. it causes over 15000 deaths each year.

12. Foodborne illness is likely to be spread by all of the following foods EXCEPT:
    a. pasteurized milk.
    b. meats.
    c. eggs.
    d. sprouts.

13. The MOST common causes of foodborne illness are:
    a. toxins and fungi.
    b. bacteria and viruses.
    c. marine organisms.
    d. viruses and fungi.

14. Which of the following is the MOST common way that bacteria and viruses enter the food supply?:
    a. Contamination of food with animal feces
    b. Hand washing
    c. Improper heating of food
    d. Improper freezing of food

15. All of the following are true regarding *Campylobacter* EXCEPT:
    a. undercooked poultry is a food commonly affected.
    b. onset is 8-10 days.
    c. symptoms include diarrhea and vomiting.
    d. it is the cause of the greatest number of cases of bacteria-related foodborne illness each year.

16. All of the following are true regarding *E. coli* 0157:H7 EXCEPT:
    a. raw or undercooked beef is a food commonly affected.
    b. onset is in 1-8 days.
    c. human feces is a usual source of contamination.
    d. symptoms include bloody diarrhea.

17. All of the following are possible sources of food contamination EXCEPT:
    a. antibiotics given to animals.
    b. hormones given to animals.
    c. pesticides.
    d. purified water.

18. All of the following are true regarding antibiotics EXCEPT:
    a. farm animals are routinely given antibiotics to increase longevity.
    b. farm animals are routinely given antibiotics to treat infectious disease.
    c. antibiotics given to animals can be the same as the ones given to humans.
    d. resistant strains of microorganisms that infect people can develop.

19. All of the following are true regarding hormones EXCEPT:
    a. hormones are given to farm-raised animals to promote growth.
    b. consumers are unconcerned about the effects.
    c. hormones are given to farm-raised animals to increase milk production.
    d. hormones given to animals show up in foods.

20. High risk groups for severe effects of foodborne illness include all of the following EXCEPT:
    a. healthy adults.
    b. young children.
    c. pregnant women.
    d. people with weakened immune systems.

21. All of the following are true regarding foodborne illnesses EXCEPT:
    a. their impact on health ranges from a day of nausea to death within minutes.
    b. over 250 types of foodborne illness have been identified.
    c. almost all cases are reported to the proper authorities.
    d. effects are most severe in the young and old.

22. All of the following are among the MOST common foodborne illnesses EXCEPT:
    a. *Salmonella*.
    b. *E. coli* 0157:H7.
    c. *Helicobacter pylori*.
    d. *Campylobacter*.

23. The bacterium that is the cause of the greatest number of foodborne illnesses each year is:
    a. *Salmonella*.
    b. *E. coli* 0157:H7.
    c. *C. botulinum*.
    d. *Campylobacter*.

24. All of the following are true regarding parasites EXCEPT:
    a. they include tapeworms, flatworms, and roundworms.
    b. they are usually killed by freezing.
    c. raw fish is a source.
    d. they are not always killed by high temperatures.

25. The two major approaches to prevention of foodborne illness include:
    a. pesticide use and irradiation.
    b. hormone use and antibiotic use.
    c. food safety regulations for processing and safe consumer behaviors.
    d. consumer behaviors and restaurant inspections.

26. All of the following are true regarding irradiation EXCEPT:
    a. it destroys bacteria.
    b. it destroys parasites.
    c. irradiated foods retain some radiation.
    d. irradiation causes texture and taste changes in some foods.

27. According to the Centers for Disease Control and Prevention, the single most important means of preventing bacterial foodborne illness is:
    a. irradiation.
    b. proper hand washing.
    c. antibiotic use.
    d. proper refrigeration.

28. Foods that should not be eaten due to the risk of contamination with microorganisms include all of the following EXCEPT:
    a. unpasteurized milk.
    b. raw eggs.
    c. raw vegetables.
    d. undercooked meats.

29. All of the following are tips for safe food handling EXCEPT:
    a. "Wash hands with soap and water before handling foods."
    b. "Do not consume foods that are past their expiration date."
    c. "When in doubt, throw it out."
    d. "Never leave perishable foods at room temperature for more than 3 hours."

30. All of the following are tips for safe food handling EXCEPT:
    a. "Avoid contact between raw and cooked foods."
    b. "Keep hot foods over 120 degrees F and cold foods below 50 degrees F."
    c. "Wash fresh fruits and vegetables thoroughly with warm water before eating."
    d. "Freeze or refrigerate leftovers promptly."

To check yourself, use the answer key at the bottom of the page.[33]

---

[33] 1. c, 2. d, 3. c, 4. b, 5. d, 6. b, 7. a, 8. a, 9. c, 10. c, 11. d, 12. a, 13. b, 14. a, 15. b, 16. c, 17. d, 18. a, 19. b, 20. a, 21. c, 22. c, 23. d, 24. d, 25. c, 26. c, 27. b, 28. c, 29. d, 30. b

Unit 33 – Aspects of Global Nutrition

Key Concepts

- The world produces enough food for all its people.
- Poverty, corrupt governments, the HIV/AIDS epidemic, low rates of breast-feeding, unsafe water supplies, and discrimination against females all contribute to malnutrition.
- Malnutrition early in life has long-term effects on mental and physical development.
- Rates of diseases such as heart disease, diabetes, and hypertension increase in developing countries that adopt Western lifestyles and eating habits.

Unit Outline

I. State of the world's health
II. Food and nutrition: The global challenge
    A. Survivors of malnutrition
        1. Malnutrition and infection
    B. Why do starvation and malnutrition happen?
    C. Ending malnutrition
        1. Success stories
        2. The World Food Summit
        3. The "nutrition transition": Rising rates of obesity and chronic diseases
    D. The future

Unit Glossary

- **marasmus:** A severe form of malnutrition primarily due to a chronic lack of calories and protein. Also called protein-energy malnutrition.
- **kwashiorkor:** A severe form of protein-energy malnutrition in young children. It is characterized by swelling, fatty liver, susceptibility to infection, profound apathy, and poor appetite. The cause of kwashiorkor is unclear.

Practice Multiple-Choice Test

1. Which of the following countries has the highest life expectancy?
    a. Zambia
    b. Russia
    c. Japan
    d. Ethiopia

2. Which of the following developing regions of the world has a rate of underweight children that is greater than 30%?
    a. South Asia
    b. Latin America
    c. North Africa
    d. East Asia

3. Of the following developing countries, where is the rate of underweight children the highest?
   a. Caribbean
   b. Sub-Saharan Africa
   c. North Africa
   d. Pacific

4. All of the following mineral deficiencies are considered priority problems in developing countries EXCEPT:
   a. iodine deficiency.
   b. iron deficiency.
   c. magnesium deficiency.
   d. zinc deficiency.

5. All of the following are true regarding marasmus EXCEPT:
   a. it is also called protein-calorie malnutrition.
   b. children with marasmus have a "moon face."
   c. children with marasmus do not get enough calories and protein in their diet.
   d. it is a type of malnutrition.

6. All of the following are true regarding kwashiorkor EXCEPT:
   a. it is a type of malnutrition.
   b. it is characterized by swelling.
   c. children with kwashiorkor do not get enough protein in their diet.
   d. children with kwashiorkor are able to readily utilize protein when well fed.

7. The main reason that people become malnourished or starve is due to:
   a. education.
   b. climate.
   c. poverty.
   d. poor agricultural practices.

8. Women and children are at particular risk for malnutrition in many countries for all of the following reasons EXCEPT:
   a. food is allocated to men and boys first.
   b. there is discrimination against women.
   c. there are sanctions against the use of birth control.
   d. women have higher nutritional needs than men.

9. The king of Thailand _____ in order to address the iodine deficiency problem in his country.
   a. issued a proclamation encouraging breast-feeding
   b. distributed packets of salt
   c. attended the World Food Summit
   d. regulated the fortification of flour

10. All of the following are true regarding breast-feeding in developing countries EXCEPT:
    a. it provides suboptimal nutrition.
    b. it contains substances that protect children from infection.
    c. low rates promote the spread of infection.
    d. use of formula prepared with contaminated water increases infection.

176

11. All of the following are true regarding global communities EXCEPT:
    a. 31 countries are considered industrialized.
    b. 113 countries are developing.
    c. the majority of the countries in the world are developing.
    d. Canada is considered a "developing" country.

12. The countries in the global community are categorized as any of the following EXCEPT:
    a. poorly developed.
    b. least developed.
    c. developing.
    d. industrialized.

13. Disparities in health status and life expectancy among countries in the global community can be attributed to all of the following EXCEPT:
    a. differences in financial resources.
    b. differences in population growth.
    c. differences in food preferences.
    d. rates of malnutrition.

14. All of the following indicators are tracked in order to monitor the general state of health of populations in various countries EXCEPT:
    a. pregnancy outcomes.
    b. rates of breast-feeding.
    c. access to the Internet.
    d. access to safe drinking water.

15. All of the following are true regarding key indicators of health status in developing countries EXCEPT:
    a. low birthweight in infants contributes to decreased longevity.
    b. underweight in children contributes to decreased longevity.
    c. lack of access to safe drinking water indicates health problems.
    d. low rates of breast-feeding indicate lack of nutritional problems.

16. Which of the following countries is classified as "industrialized"?
    a. Brazil
    b. Iceland
    c. Bahamas
    d. Haiti

17. All of the following countries are classified as "least developed" EXCEPT:
    a. Japan.
    b. Sierra Leone.
    c. Afghanistan.
    d. Ethiopia.

18. Which of the following countries has the lowest life expectancy?
    a. Japan
    b. Cuba
    c. United States
    d. Zambia

19. The health and nutrition status of populations in developing countries is monitored by all of the following organization EXCEPT the:
    a. World Health Organization (WHO).
    b. Food and Agriculture Organization (FAO).
    c. Environmental Health Organization (EHO).
    d. United Nations International Children's Emergency Fund (UNICEF).

20. Which of the following is an indictor of malnutrition?
    a. Access to safe drinking water
    b. Underweight children
    c. Exclusive breast-feeding
    d. Access to adequate healthcare

21. A type of malnutrition caused by a lack of calories and protein is called:
    a. anorexia.
    b. goiter.
    c. marasmus.
    d. bulimia.

22. How does the state of hunger and starvation affect people?
    a. It may prompt stealing or assaulting others to obtain food
    b. It speeds growth and development in children
    c. It encourages selflessness and self-sacrifice
    d. It causes temporary and mild psychological distress

23. All of the following are priority problem areas related to malnutrition in developing countries EXCEPT:
    a. low fruit and vegetable intake.
    b. alcohol abuse.
    c. overweight and obesity.
    d. high intake of whole grains.

24. All of the following are priority problem areas related to malnutrition in developing countries EXCEPT:
    a. malnutrition and increased complications from HIV/AIDS.
    b. overuse of protein supplements.
    c. lack of breastfeeding.
    d. childhood protein-calorie malnutrition.

25. Which of these vitamin deficiencies are considered priority problems in developing countries?
    a. Vitamin A and folate deficiencies
    b. Vitamin C and vitamin D deficiencies
    c. Vitamin A and vitamin D deficiencies
    d. Vitamin C and folate deficiencies

26. All of the following are true regarding the effects of malnutrition during the first 2 years of life EXCEPT:
    a. malnourished children will experience permanent delays in mental development.
    b. refeeding can reverse any effects of malnutrition during this time.
    c. the severity of the mental delays depends on the duration of malnutrition.
    d. the psychological effects can last until adulthood.

27. All of the following are true regarding the relationship between malnutrition and infection EXCEPT:
    a. malnutrition weakens the immune system.
    b. bouts of diarrhea often accompany malnutrition.
    c. poor sanitary conditions contribute to both malnutrition and infection.
    d. low rates of breast-feeding decrease the spread of infection.

28. All of the following are described as root causes of malnutrition in developing countries EXCEPT:
    a. the HIV/AIDS epidemic.
    b. equal rights for women.
    c. low levels of education.
    d. unsafe water.

29. Solutions to ending malnutrition will depend on all of the following EXCEPT:
    a. the ability of humans to work together to achieve peace.
    b. the ability of humans to work together to establish a single global language.
    c. the ability of humans to work together to achieve improved sanitation.
    d. the ability of humans to work together to achieve social equity for women and children.

30. All of the following are examples of successful efforts to reduce malnutrition EXCEPT:
    a. vitamin A supplements and education.
    b. iodization of salt.
    c. introduction of MacDonald's fast food into many developing countries.
    d. fortification of flour with iron.

To check yourself, use the answer key at the bottom of the page.[34]

---

[34] 1. c, 2. a, 3. b, 4. c, 5. b, 6. d, 7. c, 8. d, 9. b, 10. a, 11. d, 12. a, 13. c, 14. c, 15. d, 16. b, 17. a, 18. d, 19. c, 20. b, 21. c, 22. a, 23. d, 24. b, 25. a, 26. b, 27. d, 28. b, 29. b, 30. c

Worksheet 1
Family Tree Health History[35]

Fill in the table to the extent you can by placing a "✓" under any of your relatives (biological or adoptive) who have a history of the disease or disorder listed.

Disease or Disorder	Maternal Grandparents	Paternal Grandparents	Mother	Father	Brother or Sister
Hypertension					
Heart Disease/heart attack					
Cancer					
Diabetes					
Osteoporosis					
Tooth decay					

In general, the greater the number of relatives with a specific disease or disorder, the greater the likelihood that other family members may develop the same disease or disorder. It should be remembered that family history is only one of many indicators of disease risk among family members. Adoptive persons with unknown family history may have genetic characteristics that increase or decrease disease risk in ways that cannot be estimated by this activity.

[35] Resource utilized: http://cdc.gov/gemonics/info/reports/files/tables/famhist_yoon2.htm, accessed 9/02.

Names: _____

Worksheet 2
Creating Your Own Fraudulent Nutrition Product

1. Identify a common appearance, health, or vitality concern or problem that will be "fixed" by your fraudulent nutrition product.

2. Develop components of an advertisement for the product:
   A. Give the product a name, state what the product is made from (for example vitamins, fatty acids, herbs), and connect the product to a biological process in the body.

   B. Develop a scientific-sounding explanation for why the product works and refer to a scientific study that proves it does.

   C. Dream up a few testimonials, or fake "expert" statements concerning the effectiveness of the product.

   D. Include in the advertisement a money-back guarantee.

Names _____

Worksheet 3
Cultural Influences on Food Preferences Interview Form

Instructions: Begin the interview by introducing yourself (if needed). Ask your interview partner the following questions and record his or her responses. Then your partner asks you the same questions and records your answers.

1. Name a holiday that your family celebrated with a special meal: _____
2. Name two foods that were typically served at the meal.

_____   _____

3. What specific food or beverage were you given by your parent or guardian when you were young and sick with a cold, the flu, or other common childhood illness?

_____   _____

4. Name two foods that were typically served at birthday parties when you were growing up.

_____   _____

5. Will you continue some or all of these food traditions into the future?

☐ yes   ☐ no   ☐ not sure

1. Name a holiday that your family celebrated with a special meal: _____
2. Name two foods that were typically served at the meal.

_____   _____

3. What specific food or beverage were you given by your parent or guardian when you were young and sick with a cold, the flu, or other common childhood illness?

_____   _____

4. Name two foods that were typically served at birthday parties when you were growing up.

_____   _____

5. Will you continue some or all of these food traditions into the future?

☐ yes   ☐ no   ☐ not sure

Name _____

Worksheet 5
Behavioral Change Plan Activity

Instructions: Complete the assignment on this form. Do not attach pages. Steps in one approach to improving a component of dietary intake are given below. Identify a weakness in your diet identified by your dietary assessment results (low calcium intake, for example). Then think about a small, specific, and acceptable change you could make to your diet to improve your intake of that component of your diet.

1. Identify a weakness in your diet revealed by your dietary assessment results that you would like to improve.

2. Identify two foods you like that, if consumed, would strengthen the weakness identified.

3. Identify two foods you could replace in your diet to make room for the foods identified in 2.

4. State which food addition option identified in #2 would be easiest to incorporate into your diet, and which food option listed in #3 would be easiest to replace.

   Easiest food to add: Easiest food to replace:

5. Plan how to incorporate this change in your diet.
   a. When during a day would you consume the "easiest food to add"?

   b. How much of this food would you likely consume?

   c. How would you make sure this food would be available when you plan to consume it?

   d. When during a day would you normally consume the "easiest food to replace"?

   e. How much of this food would you likely replace with the food you'll be adding to your diet?

Name _____

Worksheet 7
Portion Size Recording Form

Instructions: Write down your estimate of the portion size of the foods on display using the measuring units indicated for each food.

1. Tossed salad   _____ cup(s)

2. Corn flakes   _____ cup(s) _____ ounce(s)

3. Glass of juice   _____ cup(s) _____ ounce(s)

4. Hamburger patty   _____ ounce(s)

5. Flour tortilla   _____ inches in diameter

6. Sugar packet   _____ teaspoon(s)

7. Pat of margarine   _____ teaspoon(s)

8. Cheese slice   _____ ounce(s)

9. Pasta   _____ cup(s)

10. Potato chips   _____ ounce(s)

Name _____

Worksheet 8
Dietary Assessment Assignment

Instructions: Follow these instructions carefully when completing this assignment. You will be asked to hand in your completed "Dietary Intake Recording Form," three "Nutrient Intake Results" printouts, and the completed form "Evaluation of Dietary Assessment Results."

1. Record your dietary intake for 1 weekend day and 2 week days.
   a. Try to select days that represent your usual food intake.

   b. Carry the Dietary Intake Recording Form with you during the days you will be recording your food intake.

   c. Write down foods, beverages, and ingredients in mixed dishes, and the amount of each you consumed, on the form. Fully describe each food item.

   d. Try to record your food intake after each meal or snack.

   e. To increase the accuracy of estimates of food portion sizes, refer to Nutrition Facts panels on food labels and note the weight or measure of a standard amount of the food item. (For example, a slice of cheese may be labeled as weighing an ounce.) Serve yourself foods and beverages using a cup measure, or bowls, mugs, and glasses of known volume. Estimate diameters of round foods, such as pancakes, tortillas, and bagels using a piece of 8 ½" x 11" notebook or tablet paper.

2. Review your dietary intake record for completeness.

3. To enter and analyze your dietary intake:
   a. Go to www.mypyramidtracker.gov.
   (Hint: MyPyramid Tracker can get busy and slow. *Try to avoid the peak period of usage which is from 12 noon to 4 p.m. EST Monday through Thursday. It may take an hour to complete this analysis.*)

   b. Select "Assess Your Food Intake."

   c. Log in, complete personal profile, and select "Proceed to Food Intake."

   d. Enter food items one at a time from your dietary intake record. When you have finished entering the foods, check to make sure you have entered all of them and made no entry mistakes.

   e. After all foods have been entered correctly, go to "Select Quantity" on the right-hand side of the screen.

   f. Indicate the appropriate quantity of each food entered.

g. When all quantities have been entered and reviewed for accuracy, click the "Print Food Record" words and make a copy to hand in. Then click the "Save & Analyze" button.

h. From the "Analyze Your Food Intake" page, select "Nutrient Intakes." Print a copy of the Nutrient Intakes results to hand in.

i. Repeat the above process to enter and analyze your dietary intake for the two other days.

4. Complete the Evaluation of Dietary Assessment Results form.

5. Prepare to hand in your assignment by stapling together your Dietary Intake Recording Form, copies of the Food Record that show types and amounts of foods entered for the 3 days, your three Nutrient Intakes printouts, and the Evaluation of Dietary Assessment Results form.

Evaluation of Dietary Assessment Results

Instructions: Use the results from the Nutrient Intakes printouts to complete the following activities.

1. Calculate your average intake of Calories (kcal) for the three days.
   Example: Food Energy (kcal): Day 1 = 2310, Day 2 = 1990, Day 3 = 2250;
   2310 + 1990 + 2250 = 6550 kcal
   6550 kcal/3 = 2183 kcal per day

   Your average, total energy (kcal) intake per day (show all calculations):

   _____ **kcal per day**

2. Calculate the average percentage of Calories from carbohydrate for the three days.

   a. Add daily results for Carbohydrate (g) intake. Multiply this total times 4 Calories per gram. Then, divide the total by 3 to get an average intake of Calories from carbohydrate for one day.
   Example: carbohydrate (g) Day 1 = 191, Day 2 = 78, Day 3 = 245;
   191 + 202 + 245 = 638 g
   638 g x 4 kcal/g = 2552 kcal
   2552 Calories /3 = 851 Calories (kcal) from carbohydrate per day

Your results (show all calculations):

_____ **kcal from carbohydrate per day**

b. Divide your average, daily intake of Calories from carbohydrate by your average, daily total energy (kcal) intake. Multiply the result by 100 to obtain the percentage.
Example: 851 / 2183 kcal = 0.32;
        0.32 x 100 = 39% total energy (kcal) from carbohydrate

Your results (show all calculations):

_____% **total energy (kcal) from carbohydrate**

3. Calculate the average percentage of Calories from protein for the three days:

a. Add daily results for protein (g) intake. Multiply this total times 4 Calories per gram. Then, divide the total by 3 to get an average intake of Calories from protein for one day.

Your results (show all calculations):

_____ **kcal from protein per day**

b. Divide your average, daily intake of Calories from protein by your average, daily total energy (kcal) intake. Multiply the result by 100 to obtain the percentage.

Your results (show all calculations):

_____% **total energy (kcal) from protein**

192

4. Calculate the average percentage of Calories from fat in your diet:

a. Add daily results for total fat (g) intake from the three Nutrient Intakes printouts. Multiply this total times 9 Calories per gram. Then, divide the total by 3 to get an average intake of Calories from fat for one day.

   Your results (show all calculations):

   _____ kcal from total fat per day

b. Divide your average, daily intake of Calories from fat by your average, daily total energy (kcal) intake. Multiply the result by 100 to obtain the percentage.

   Your results (show all calculations):

   _____% total energy (kcal) from fat

5. Add the average, daily percent of Calories from carbohydrate, protein, and fat together.

   Your results (show the calculation):

a. Does the result add up to 100%?   ☐ yes   ☐ no

b. If the sum is not 100%, and your calculation is off by more than 2%, recalculate the percentages of Calories from carbohydrate, protein, and fat. The percentages should be 100% or within a percent or two of 100%.

6. Calculate the average percentage of Calories from saturated fat in your diet:

a. Add daily results for saturated fat (g) intake from the three Nutrient Intakes printouts. Multiply this total times 9 Calories per gram. Then, divide the total by 3 to get an average intake of Calories from saturated fat for one day.

Your results (show all calculations):

_____ kcal from saturated fat per day

b. Divide your average daily intake of Calories from saturated fat by your average daily total energy (kcal) intake. Multiply the result by 100 to obtain the percentage.

Your results (show all calculations):

_____% of Calories (kcal) from saturated fat

7. Calculate the percent of Calories (kcal) from mono- and polyunsaturated fats in your average daily diet by subtracting your percent of Calories (kcals) from saturated fat from the percent of Calories (kcal) consumed from fat.

Your results (show all calculations):

_____% of Calories (kcal) from mono- and polyunsaturated fats

8. Calculate your average, daily intake of cholesterol.

Your results (show all calculations):

_____ mg cholesterol per day

194

9. Complete the following table:

   a. Record your average, daily intake of food energy (kcal), and the percent of Calories from carbohydrate, protein, fat, saturated fat, and mono- and polyunsaturated fat determined previously in the table below.
   b. Record average daily cholesterol intake previously determined.
   c. Record daily potassium and sodium intake in mg, then calculate and record average daily intake in mg.
   d. Record the percent figures in the Percent of Recommended Intake column (the third column) on the Nutrient Intakes printout to fill in the blanks for vitamins and minerals. Calculate and record average daily percent of recommended intakes (% rec) for each vitamin and mineral listed in the table.

	Percent of Recommended Intake			Average Daily Intake
	Day 1	Day 2	Day 3	
Food energy (kcal)				
Protein (% kcal)				
Carbohydrate (% kcal)				
Dietary fiber (%)				
Total fat (% kcal)				
Saturated fat (% kcal)				
Mono- and polyunsaturated fat (% kcal)				
Cholesterol (mg)				
Vitamin A (% rec)				
Vitamin E (% rec)				
Vitamin C (% rec)				
Thiamin (% rec)				
Riboflavin (% rec)				
Niacin (% rec)				
Folate (% rec)				
Vitamin B_6 (% rec)				
Vitamin B_{12} (% rec)				
Calcium (% rec)				

	Percent of Recommended Intake			Average Daily Intake
	Day 1	Day 2	Day 3	
Iron (% rec)				
Magnesium (% rec)				
Phosphorus (% rec)				
Zinc (% rec)				
Potassium (mg)				
Sodium (mg)				

10. List two strong points of your diet based on the results of your dietary analysis.

a. _____   b. _____

11. List two weak points of your diet based on the results of your dietary analysis.

a. _____   b. _____

12. Answer the following questions about your average daily dietary intakes.

a. Does your intake of protein exceed 100% of the recommended intake?

☐ yes   ☐ no

b. Does the percentage of Calories you consume from total fat fall within the recommended range of 20-35% of total Calories?

☐ yes   ☐ no

c. Is the percentage of Calories you consume from saturated fat less than the recommended limit of 7% of total Calories?

☐ yes   ☐ no

d. Do you consume over 300 mg of cholesterol daily?

☐ yes   ☐ no

196

e. Does your average daily intake of potassium fall within the range of 3,525 - 5,875 mg? (The DRI is 4,700 mg per day.)

☐ yes   ☐ no

f. Is your average daily intake of sodium less than 2,300 mg? (The DRI is 1,500 mg per day.)

☐ yes   ☐ no

g. List the vitamins consumed in amounts over twice the recommended intake level:

h. List vitamins consumed in amounts under 75% of the recommended intake level:

i. List minerals consumed in amounts over twice the recommended intake level:

j. List minerals consumed in amounts under 75% of the recommended intake level:

Prepare your forms for submission (see point 5 of the Dietary Assessment instructions).

Congratulations! You have completed your dietary assessment.

Dietary Intake Recording Form – Day _____

Food/Beverage	Description	Quantity

Dietary Intake Recording Form – Day _____

Food/Beverage	Description	Quantity

Dietary Intake Recording Form – Day _____

Food/Beverage	Description	Quantity

Dietary Intake Recording Form – Day _____

Food/Beverage	Description	Quantity

Name_____

Worksheet 9
Physical Activity Assessment

Instructions:

1. On the form below, record the types of physical activities you perform in a usual day, including sleeping. Carefully estimate in minutes the amount of time you spent actively engaged in each activity. The total number of minutes recorded must equal 1,440 (24 hours). A usual day's physical activities can be reasonably well represented by the activities you undertake 4 or more times a week. Say you jog every weekday but swim twice a week. The jogging would be included in your activity log but the swimming would not be.

2. Access the Physical Activity Tool:
    a. Go to www.mypyramidtracker.gov and select "Assess Your Physical Activity." From there:
    b. Login
    c. Complete Personal Profile and then select "Proceed to Physical Activity."
    d. From the Physical Activity Tool page, select "Standard Option."
    e. Under "Enter Activity Type" enter each of the activities performed and then go to "Select Duration" on the right-hand side of the page. Enter the amount of time you spent in each activity listed.
    f. When finished entering time spent in each physical activity, select the option "Save & Analyze."
    g. From the "Analyze Your Physical Activity" page select "Physical Activity Assessment."
    h. Review your results summary.
    i. Print a copy of "Your Physical Activity Results."

3. Staple a copy of "Your Physical Activity Results" printout to this form before you submit the assignment to your instructor.

Usual Day's Physical Activities

Type of Activity	Duration[a] (minutes)	Type of Activity	Duration (minutes)

[a] Total minutes must add up to 1,440.

Name _____

Worksheet 10
Anthropometry Lab

A. Use the best estimate of your current height and weight to calculate your Body Mass Index (BMI); or, alternatively, calculate the BMI of the hypothetical adult in question 4.

Calculating BMI from Your Estimated Height and Weight

1. What is your height without shoes? Round the measurement to the nearest quarter inch (e.g. 0.25, 0.50, or 0.75 inches). _____ feet _____._____ inches

2. What is your weight without clothing? _____ pounds

3. Based on your estimated height and weight, what is your BMI? _____ kg/m²

$$BMI = \frac{\text{Weight in pounds}}{(\text{Height in inches}) \times (\text{height in inches})} \times 703 \quad \text{(Show calculations.)}$$

or Calculating BMI for a Hypothetical Adult

4. Calculate BMI for a hypothetical adult who reports that his height is 6 feet, 3 inches, and his weight is 220 pounds. (Show calculations)

BMI = _____ kg/m²

B. Measuring Stations

Height

1. Take a turn being measured and helping another student be measured. As a helper, ensure that the student being measured and the right angle board are in the proper positions for the measurement.

2. Height is measured without shoes (socks are okay) while a person is standing with his or her back at the center of the measuring tape. The person should be:
   a. Flat on their feet with heels almost together,
   b. Looking straight ahead, and

204

c. Positioned so that shoulder blades, buttocks, and heels are touching the measurement surface (see the illustration below[36]).

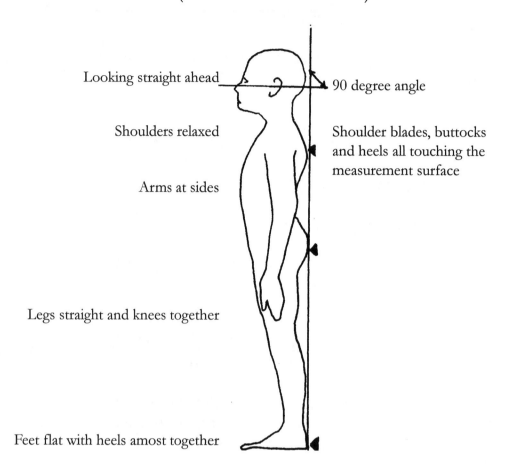

Looking straight ahead — 90 degree angle

Shoulders relaxed

Shoulder blades, buttocks and heels all touching the measurement surface

Arms at sides

Legs straight and knees together

Feet flat with heels amost together

3. When the person is in this position:
   a. Place one flat surface of the right angle board on the top of the middle of the person's head, and the other flat surface directly against the measuring wall.
   b. Lightly press the angle board down on the person's head to flatten hair if needed.
   c. Draw a line that follows the base of the right angle board to the measuring tape and read the measurement.
   d. Round the measurement to the nearest quarter inch (e.g. 0.25, 0.50, or 0.75 inches).

4. What is your measured height?   _____ feet _____._____ inches

---

[36] CDC, government publication.

5. Recalculate your BMI if your measured height is different than the height estimated for question A1. If the height figures are the same, complete question 6 below. (Show calculations)

_____ kg/m²   *or...*

6. Recalculate BMI for the hypothetical adult who is measured to be 6 feet, 1.5 inches tall but still weighs 220 pounds. (Show calculations)

_____ kg/m²

Waist Circumference

7. a. Measure your waist circumference while in light, indoor clothing if possible.
   b. Place the measuring tape around the smallest circumference below the last rib of the rib cage and above the navel. The tape should be flat against your waist and level.
   c. Take your measurement of waist circumference where the beginning of the tape meets the part of the tape you have placed around your waist.

Name _____

Worksheet 12
Assessing Calcium Intake

Instructions: Enter the number of servings of foods listed that you usually consume in a day, and calculate the milligrams of calcium consumed from the foods (see example). Then add the results in the "Total Calcium" column to get an estimated total of your calcium intake. Subtract your total from the AI of 1,000 mg per day to estimate how close your calcium intake is to the AI for calcium.

Example:

Food	Serving Size	Number of Servings	Calcium/ Serving (mg)[37]	Calcium (mg)
Orange juice, calcium fortified	1 cup	1 ½	x 300 =	450
			Total =	450

Yogurt	1 cup		x 400 =	
Pudding made with milk	1 cup		x 300 =	
Orange juice, calcium fortified	1 cup		x 300 =	
Milk (cow's, or calcium-fortified soy or rice)	1 cup		x 300 =	
Tofu, processed with calcium	½ cup		x 300 =	
Sesame seeds	1 ounce		x 300 =	
Cheese	1 ounce		x 200 =	
Ice cream	1 cup		x 200 =	
Collard greens	½ cup		x 150 =	
Cottage cheese	1 cup		x 150 =	
Green soybeans, cooked	½ cup		x 130 =	
Tahini	2 tablespoons		x 130 =	
Almonds	¼ cup		x 100 =	
			Subtotal =	

[37] Values are rounded and in some cases average values for food types are given.

208

Food	Serving Size	Number of Servings	Calcium/ Serving (mg)[38]	Calcium (mg)
		Subtotal from other side =		
Dried beans, cooked	1 cup		x 100 =	
Turnip greens, cooked	½ cup		x 100 =	
Soy nuts	¼ cup		x 100 =	
Bok choy, cooked	½ cup		x 80 =	
Tempeh	½ cup		x 80 =	
Kale, cooked	½ cup		x 80 =	
Okra, cooked	½ cup		x 70 =	
Broccoli, cooked	½ cup		x 50 =	
Swiss chard, cooked	½ cup		x 50 =	
Tortilla, 6" diameter	1		x 50 =	
			Total =	

AI for calcium = 1,000 mg
Total = _____ mg
Difference (subtract total from AI) = _____ mg

[38] Values are rounded and in some cases average values for food types are given.

Worksheet 13
Should Herbs Be Regulated as Drugs?

Scenario: You are a consumer member of an FDA subcommittee that will provide the FDA with consumer views on whether herbal remedies should be regulated as drugs and not as food. Drugs have to pass tests related to their safety and effectiveness before they can be sold to prevent or treat disease. You are asked to prepare your responses to the following questions before the first meeting of the subcommittee takes place. What would your responses be?

A. Have you used herbal remedies to prevent or treat a disease? ☐ yes ☐ no

   If yes, did you consider the herbal remedy to be a drug or a food? ☐ food ☐ drug

B. State 3 reasons why herbal remedies should not be regulated as drugs.

   1.

   2.

   3.

C. State 3 reasons why herbal remedies should be regulated as drugs.

   1.

   2.

   3.

D. Should testing the safety and effectiveness of herbal products be required before they are sold to the public? ☐ yes ☐ no

   Why or why not?

E. Would you feel the right to freedom of speech would be compromised if herbal remedies were regulated as drugs? ☐ yes ☐ no

   Why or why not?

Worksheet 15A
Child Nutrition Dilemmas 1

Instructions: Consider the scenarios presented and answer the questions posed. Base your responses on the information presented in the section "How Do Food Preferences Develop" and other information presented in Unit 30.

Scenario 1: Lola is almost 3 years old and her parents want to introduce her to a variety of new foods. Tonight at dinner they decide to serve Lola beets for the first time. Lola eats the mashed potatoes and chicken that were on her plate, but she doesn't touch the beets. What should you do?

Develop 3 optional responses to the dilemma:

a.

b.

c.

Identify the worst option and state why it is the worst one.

Identify the best option and state why it is the best one.

212

Scenario 2: Your 4-year-old son comes into the kitchen announcing he's hungry and asks for a cookie. Dinner is an hour away and you don't want him to spoil his appetite. What should you do?

Develop 3 optional responses to the dilemma:

a.

b.

c.

Identify the worst option and state why it is the worst one.

Identify the best option and state why it is the best one.

Worksheet 15B
Child Nutrition Dilemmas 2

Instructions: Consider the scenarios presented and answer the questions posed. Base your responses on the information presented in the section "How Do Food Preferences Develop" and other information presented in Unit 30.

Scenario 3: It's Friday night and Elesha and Raymond are excited. Their parents are taking them to the "Country Cookin' Buffet" for dinner. On the way to the restaurant their dad lets the kids know that they can choose foods from the buffet they like, but that they should eat all the food they take. Elesha and Raymond take too much food and can't eat it all. If you were the dad, what should you do?

Develop 3 optional responses to the dilemma:

a.

b.

c.

Identify the worst option and state why it is the worst one.

Identify the best option and state why it is the best one.

Scenario 4: It's Saturday afternoon and the proud parents of 6-month-old Elena are busy playing with her on the floor. After about 10 minutes of playing, Elena starts to fuss and then she cries. Her parents don't know what's wrong, but decide she must be hungry and feed her. What would you have done?

Develop 3 optional responses to the dilemma:

a.

b.

c.

Identify the worst option and state why it is the worst one.

Identify the best option and state why it is the best one.